STOCK MARKET INTELLIGENCE

JEFF LUKE

CONTENTS

Disclaimer   vii

Quote   viii

Part I   1

1. You Got This   3
2. Accelerate Your Learning   5
3. What Do You Understand?   7

Part II   15

4. The Palms Filter   17
5. P For Profitable   20
6. A For Adaptable   31
7. L For Loyal   35
8. M For Moat   43
9. S For Sensible Price   49
10. Use Your Own PALMS Filter   63

Part III   65

11. A New Way   67
12. How To Invest Today   70
13. What Is A Stock?   76
14. Find Your Edge   79
15. Buffett On His Edge   85
16. What Do You Understand?   92
17. Focus Is Key   98
18. A Good Checklist   101
19. A Reliable System   105

Part IV   113

20. The Magic Box   115
21. Eye On Eternity   120
22. Ideas From Great Investors   125
23. We're All Indexers   128

24. My Investing Mistakes … 131

25. A Calm Captain … 146

26. If … 149

27. The Antifragile Investor … 153

28. Cheap Stock Trades … 162

29. Robinhood Dreams … 166

30. Equanimity … 171

31. Patience … 174

32. Decisiveness … 177

33. Price Is What You Pay … 180

34. Your inner scorecard … 183

35. Buffett And Munger's Filters … 186

36. You Don't Need A Genius I.Q … 188

37. Zero-Based Thinking … 190

38. Keep It Simple … 198

39. Three Ways To Succeed … 204

40. Experimental, New And Exciting … 207

Part V … 209

41. Thought Into Action … 211

42. Decisive On Amazon … 213

43. Amazon One Year Later … 220

44. Thank you … 222

Connect … 225

About the Author … 227

Also by Jeff Luke … 229

Notes … 233

STOCK MARKET INTELLIGENCE

Investing Made Easy

JEFF LUKE

Copyright © 2020 Jeff Luke

All rights reserved.

Printed in the United States of America by Amazon.com / Kindle Direct Publishing

Permission to reproduce or transmit in any form or by any means—electronic or mechanical, including photocopying and recording—or by information storage or retrieval, must be obtained by contacting the author via email at jlukephoto@gmail.com

Ordering Information

For additional copies purchase on amazon.com or email jlukephoto@gmail.com

or by phone at (206) 778-4424. Quantity discounts are available.

Library of Congress Cataloging-in-Publication Data

Luke, Jeff, 1968-

Stock Market Intelligence: Investing Made Easy / Jeff Luke

Pages cm

Includes Index.

1. Investing 2. Stock Market. I. Luke, Jeff. II. Title

ISBN: 9781976928345

First Edition, Fourth printing June 2020

DISCLAIMER

The material in this book is for informational purposes only. Nothing in this book constitutes an offer or solicitation of financial advice and is not intended to provide investment, legal, tax, or other professional or financial advice.

Nothing in this book is to be construed as an offer or a recommendation to buy or sell a security. Additionally, the material in this book does not constitute a representation that the investments described herein are suitable or appropriate for any person.

Such content therefore should not be relied upon for the making of any personal financial and investment decisions. Persons accessing this information are strongly encouraged to obtain appropriate professional advice before making any investment or financial decision.

Disclosure: The author owns stock in Amazon, Berkshire Hathaway, Carmax, and Waters.

Before investing, please follow these simple guidelines:

1. Never invest in something that you don't understand.
2. Never invest based on anyone else's opinion.
3. Ask for assistance if you need it.

"I'm always doing things I can't do. That's how I get to do them."

— PICASSO

For my dad
My mom
Warren
Steve
Seth
Sam
Jay
Pia
Lisa
Mira
Mark
Chris
Kevin
Eddie
Shantii
Maximus
Khunploy
And my reader

PART I

YOU GOT THIS

YOU GOT THIS

Y ou shouldn't be scared.

Everyone can do well in the stock market. You have the skills, the smarts, and you don't need a fancy college degree. All you need is patience, the time to do a little research, and you've got it. Don't worry about it, don't panic.

I can help you invest better.

You can't learn everything about stock picking in one book. But you have better stock-picking skills than you realize. And you have advantages that no one on Wall Street has. I'm here to help you find and use them.

Before you start to invest, ask yourself one question: When will I need to use this money? You should only invest money in the stock market that you will not need for a long time. In the short term, the stock market is volatile, and individual stocks are volatile. A stock can range 50% between its high and its low in just one year. Stocks go up and down, so if you have a one- or two-year time horizon you shouldn't invest in stocks because there's no telling what will happen in the short term. The stock market is a great long-term investment for any money you're willing to put in the market and leave there for five, 10, 20, or 30 years.

If you need to use the money anytime soon, you should not invest in stocks. If you have to pay for car repairs, if you have credit card debt, if you need the money for rent, or to pay tuition for a kid headed to college next year — you should not have that money in the stock market.

If you're worried about investing in the stock market, don't do it. Not everybody is cut out to be an investor. Investing requires patience and the ability to remain cool under pressure. If you think you'll panic and sell your investments when the market goes down, you should not invest in stocks.

Don't be intimidated — you just need the right temperament and a useful system to pick stocks and you'll be on your way.

ACCELERATE YOUR LEARNING

The book you're reading right now is a powerful tool.

If you're just getting started, or if you've been at it a while and your results have not been as good as you hoped, this book will provide you with a system that will help.

Accelerate your learning

The system I teach will help you concentrate on a few great companies. It will accelerate your learning and help you filter out the noise and focus on what matters.

A five-step filtering system

This simple approach gives you five questions to ask before buying stock, and each one is easy to remember because it begins with the letters in the acronym "PALMS."

My goal is to teach you how to use this system quickly and easily. I think you can learn it in 15 minutes.

When you start to ask the five PALMS questions you will begin to understand the secrets of the great investors. How do I know they use them? Because they say so.[1] Why doesn't everyone use them? They're too simple.[2]

With this system, you will see how easily you can make a list of great companies and develop a sense of confidence that comes with understanding these businesses. If you spend about 15 minutes learning this system you will gain an enormous advantage over other investors. You will have a stock filtering system you can use whenever you need it.

I'm confident this system will help you as an investor. If you have questions please send me an email at jlukephoto@gmail.com and I'll try to answer them.

Thank you for taking the time to read this book. I hope it helps you succeed as an investor. I know this system works because I use it myself, and at the end of this book I will give you an example of how I used it to pick one stock that I still own today.

This book will put you on the path to investing success. Remember, if you believe you can do something, I guarantee you can do it.

WHAT DO YOU UNDERSTAND?

Before you apply the PALMS filter you will need a list of companies that you understand. It's okay if you don't know everything about each company, but you want to have an edge over most other investors you need to gain an advantage that comes from your knowledge.

For example, I was interested in biology in high school and was a bio major in college, so I am drawn to companies in the medical device, pharmaceutical, scientific measurement, and technology sectors, and I consider these all within my circle of competence: that's my edge.

You have to figure out your circle of competence and stick to it. If you try to understand too many companies or stocks you will wind up not knowing any of them very well.

All great investors know some area deeply and they stick to what they know. They become learning machines capable of reading and absorbing information and developing a deep understanding of companies. They want to know which companies are better than others, and why. Similarly, you should be able to state clearly why one company is dominant in its industry and another is second-best.

This will help you because in tough times the strong companies continue to grow and innovate while others struggle.

Sitting on your ass and focusing for long periods will be an asset in this regard. Being distracted and multitasking is your enemy.

Your first task is to make a list of companies you understand. If you don't have very deep knowledge in any area just be patient with yourself; you can take your time and learn more in the future.

To get started write down the names of between one and 10 companies.

COMPANIES YOU UNDERSTAND:

1.
2.
3.
4.
5.
6.
7.
8.
9.
10.

If you prefer not to make a list, you might want to draw a circle and write the names of companies inside the circle. The circle does not have to be large, nor does it have to contain many companies.

It doesn't matter how many companies you know. All that matters is a deep understanding of a few great businesses. Also, you should think of yourself as an investigative reporter, a curious person who always wants to know more about the company. Remember, you're buying a part of the business, and you plan to own it for a long time. So it's your job to investigate and make sure you know what's going on.

For example, I just read a press release from Waters Corporation, a company whose stock I own. The release said was titled "Waters Corporation Announces CEO Succession Plan[1]" and it announced a succession plan but named no successor. The release explained that the current CEO will step down when a successor is appointed. This is a real head-scratcher because the company made the effort to issue a press release that lacked substance.

These moves catch my attention because I want to know why the CEO is leaving. Did they get fired for poor performance? Were they hired elsewhere? Is the company struggling with weak leadership? In my experience, the vacuum created by a CEO's departure is rarely good for a company.

I immediately went to the Water's website, found the contact phone number for investor relations, and called. Why wait around when it's your money on the line? If you want to be a great investor you have to act like an investigative reporter. Otherwise, you can sit around like a sheep and wait for things to happen, but I believe that approach yields average returns.

I share this brief anecdote because it's your job as an investor to get as much information as you can about any company in which you invest. Ideally, you will own your stocks forever, but sometimes the world is less than ideal and often leadership changes can fundamentally harm a company and its stock.

I'd estimate that 95% of investors are not deeply committed. They buy the hot stocks that everyone's talking about online, and they focus on stocks that have been going up for a long time. These same investors lose money when that stock suddenly crash back to earth because no profits were backing up the sky-high stock price.

I want you to know what you're buying. I want you to be in the 5% that thinks like an owner of a company. This will protect you because you'll be on top of any changes when a new CEO takes over, or if there is instability in the company or industry. When you own stock you're an owner, and you must know the company intimately. If you don't dig for information to find out what's happening, who do you think will do it for you? How can you expect to be anything better than the average? This book gives you the tools to gain a deep under-standing before you invest.

You should have a firm grasp on which companies are leading the way in an industry and which ones are struggling. If you don't yet know a lot about all major competitors right now that's okay, but you must be on your way to becoming an expert in that industry. *Investing tends to move money from people who know little to those who know a lot.*

To give you an idea of how few companies you need to under-stand well, one of the best investors alive is Charlie Munger, and he owns three stocks: Berkshire Hathaway, Costco, and investments in Himalaya Capital, run by an intelligent Chinese investor named Li Lu. *Munger has almost all of his money in just three investments*, and dribs and drabs in a few others. I point this out to show that you don't need to own many stocks as long as you understand them well.

The purpose of making your list is not only the practice of finding great businesses but in eliminating those that can hurt your returns. You need to ignore a friend's hot stock tip, a YouTuber telling you about a stock they think is about to take off, and that email from Motley Fool telling you about the next big thing.

While some people genuinely want to help you learn, others are aiming to grab your attention to grow their channels or persuade you to buy their courses. Skilled content creators are great at persuasion, but they are not necessarily great investors. I enjoy YouTube videos, and I learn a lot from many of them, but I want to remind you that your stock decisions should be made based on company's you under-stand and not from anyone else's picks.

A stock is *part of a company*, not a ticker symbol that flashes red and green all day long. When you think of yourself *as a part-owner of a company* you will think more carefully before you invest. You'll improve your chances for success if you buy and hold quality and don't try to jump in and out of the market.

Examples of companies I understand

Warren Buffett refers to the area where you have deep knowledge as your "circle of competence" and suggests you concentrate only on stocks that fall within this circle.

"You don't have to be an expert on every company or even many. You only have to be able to evaluate companies within your circle of competence. The size of that circle is not very important; knowing its boundaries, however, is vital".[2] *— Warren Buffett*

I'll share a list of stocks that I understand, or that I'm learning about rapidly. Your list will surely be different than mine because our work, education, and experiences are different.

Here are seven companies I understand well:

1. Adobe
2. Amazon
3. Berkshire Hathaway
4. Carmax
5. Starbucks
6. Waters Corporation
7. Zoom Video Communications

In the future, I will investigate many other companies, and eventually, they will fall within my circle of competence. I have a strong interest in cloud computing companies, and those that offer software as a service (SAAS) and one of the companies above, Zoom, fits into this category. I continue to deepen my knowledge in that area. All you need is one stock to start, and it is much better to understand one company well than own 20 of them and not know any well.

Many other companies interest me, *but they do not fall within my circle of competence.* Here are examples of 20 companies in this category:

Abbvie, Agilent, Alibaba, Alnylam Pharmaceuticals, AstraZeneca,

AutoNation, Beyond Meat, Constellation Brands, Exact Sciences, Facebook, Fanuc, Ferrari, Fiat Chrysler, Ford, Gilead Sciences, GoPro, JetBlue, L Brands, LuLulemon, Nektar Therapeutics, Novartis, Nvidia, Restoration Hardware, Ping An Insurance, Sony, Square, Tencent, Thermo Fisher Scientific, and Twitter.

I believe you will *get much better returns* investing in stocks you understand and skipping over the others. You are buying parts of businesses and the better grasp you have of their competitive strengths within their industries and their long-term prospects, the more likely you'll make smart decisions.

Charlie Munger explains that part of being wise is having an awareness of the limits of your knowledge. "It's not a competency if you don't know the edge of it," he said. *"You are a disaster* if you don't know the edge of your competency.[3]"

Buying an apartment or farm

Before we proceed I think it's important to distinguish between investing and gambling. I will give you a quick overview here, and we'll dig deeper in a moment.

Gamblers and short-term traders *focus on the price.* They just want to get a quick profit and try to get out ahead of others. *Investors focus on what the business produces* over time.

Short-term traders focus on price

Gamblers and short-term traders focus on the price movement of the stock. They are concerned with whether the price moves up or down, and they spend time trying to predict its movement and make forecasts. Traders try to buy or sell a stock at just the right time to lock in a profit. They don't care about long-term prospects because they won't own the stock in five years.

Investors focus on what the asset produces

Investors want to know how much money the asset will generate over many years. When they buy stock in a company they become a part-owner of that business. The investor cares about the business income just like the owner of an apartment building cares about the rental income. How much money will they collect from tenants in rent, what's the likelihood tenants pay rent on time, and how long will it take for the owner to finish paying off the mortgage on the building?

The same goes for a farm. If you were a farmer you'd want to figure out how much alfalfa, milk, corn, wheat, eggs, or cheese your farm will produce, and how much you will earn when you sell them. An investor looking to buy the farm will *focus on what that asset will produce* over many years.

The reason you invest in stocks is *to get more money back in the future than you paid when you bought the stock*. The company can make you wealthier in three ways:

1. The company can reinvest its profits, which are called "retained earnings" because the company reinvests in computers, employees, logistics, technology, vehicles, warehouses, etc. Retained earnings can make the company much more valuable over time if they are carried out intelligently.

2. The company can buy back its stock when the price of the stock is far below the value of the shares purchased. If a company does buybacks at cheap prices it *creates value* for shareholders, but if it pays too high a price when buying back it wastes money and *destroys value*. Company executives frequently pay too much for their company's stock when carrying out share buybacks. One reason is that executive compensation is often linked to increases in earnings per share. The CEO and executives benefit from buybacks, which reduce the number of shares outstanding and increase earnings per share.

3. The company can distribute earnings to shareholders as a dividend.

I want you to be part of the small cohort of investors who get better returns than average, but you have to keep in mind that admission to this club is not free. You have to spend time figuring out which companies you truly understand, and determining with high probability if those companies will not only survive but will generate profits for years to come.

You can get rich through a few smart investments where the executives make a few high-quality decisions each year. You can just sit back and let the company increase profits, and your stock will usually increase in value too. If you buy stock in a company that makes stupid acquisitions or has leadership problems you'll find yourself enduring an endless string of frustrations as a deteriorating company coupled with a falling stock price require you to sell.

This book encourages you to say "no" when looking at many "so-so" or poorly run companies so you can concentrate your efforts on the great ones.

Once you have created your list of companies you will be ready to run them through the PALMS filtering system that we examine in the next chapter.

PART II

THE PALMS FILTER: LEARN THE FIVE INVESTING FACTORS

THE PALMS FILTER

Introducing the PALMS Filtering System

The letters of the word "PALMS" stand for investing factors. *Ask yourself these five questions:*

- Profitable - Is the company profitable?
- Adaptable - Is the company adapting to changing technology?
- Loyal Customers - Are customers devoted to the company's brand?
- Moat - Does the company possess a durable competitive advantage?
- Sensible Price - Is the stock selling at a price that makes sense?

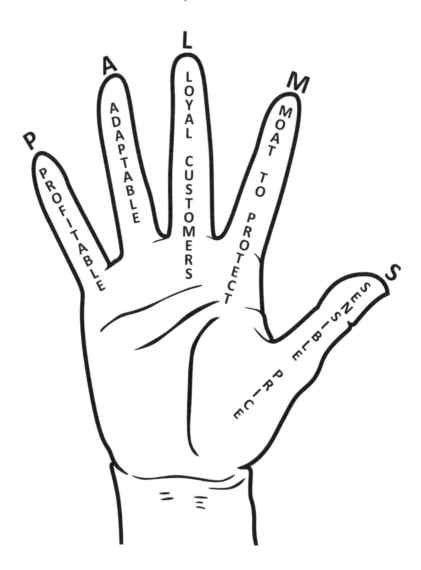

In the last chapter, you listed the stocks you understand. Now you need to figure out if those stocks make sense as investments. This method requires your answers to five basic questions.

These are not hard questions to answer, but you need to know where to look to find the answers, and I'll show you how to use the PALMS filtering system to eliminate poor investment ideas and focus on the good ones.

I believe that the PALMS filtering system helps an investor to take a rational, businesslike approach in contrast to the speculative approach that is more like gambling.

What happens when we flip it?

Let us test the PALMS filtering system by seeing what we get if we flip the system and inverted our selection criteria.

What kind of company do you get if you invert the PALMS system?

NOT Profitable - The company is losing money.

NOT Adaptable - The company is not adapting to new technologies.

NOT Loyal - Customers do not feel a strong connection to the brand.

NO Moat - The company has no durable competitive advantage and is therefore vulnerable to competition.

NOT a sensible price - The stock is too expensive.

A company displaying these characteristics would be a disaster. So, we must not ignore the power of these five factors and their impact on stock selection. This test by inverting proves the utility of each PALMS filter.

P FOR PROFITABLE

Is the company profitable?

Only consider buying stock in profitable companies. Yes, there are many exciting unprofitable companies that you can consider, but I want to help you pass over the "not yet profitable" ones and invest only in companies that are already successful. I want your investments to grow in value over time. I do not want you to have to wait for struggling companies to turn themselves around (unlikely to happen) or upstart companies to prove they can eventually turn a profit; those are both speculations, or bets based on the hope that things will work out. I want to steer you away from speculation and toward investing.

Yes, it's exciting to be an early investor in a stock that everyone is talking about. You could own Beyond Meat, Slack, Snapchat, Tesla, Uber, or any other hot stock that everyone is buying at insanely high prices, but the problem with these "hot stocks" is that for every company that will succeed, several will fail. It is difficult to tell the winners from the losers ahead of time. If you pay too much to buy a hot stock there is a good chance it will decline rapidly in price and you may never break even. The number one rule in investing is "don't lose money."

With investing, the good news is that you don't have to hit the ball over the fence every time. You just have to pick companies that are already profitable, already growing and you get to profit along with them for many years. There are fewer sleepless nights, less stress, and less hoping that your luck will change. That's all part of the gambling or speculating mindset. That is why I encourage you to skip over the not-yet-profitable companies and invest in those that are already a success.

When you're starting, I want you to avoid buying stocks that you hope will one day make money but are not yet profitable. Stick to stocks with proven track records.

Stick with big, easy decisions

Buffett made a bet that a low-cost S&P 500 index fund would beat the returns of the best and brightest hedge fund managers over 10 years. He won the bet by a landslide, and he said the final lesson from the bet is to "Stick with big, 'easy' decisions and eschew activity[1]."

In describing the wager, Buffett said, "During the 10-year-bet, the 200-plus hedge-fund managers that were involved almost certainly made tens of thousands of buy and sell decisions. Most of those managers undoubtedly thought hard about their decisions, each of which they believed would prove advantageous. In the process of investing, they studied 10-Ks, interviewed managements, read trade journals, and conferred with Wall Street analysts."

Buffett's point was that the best and brightest with their college degrees and analyses can't beat the passively managed S&P 500. Fortunately for you, you don't have to satisfy hedge fund clients, you don't have to generate returns for anyone but yourself. You have advantages that Wall Street investors don't have, namely the first-hand knowledge you have as a customer and observer of your friends and family and their purchasing habits. You may understand some companies better than Wall Street professionals.

For example, I could have made some better stock purchases ten years ago if I had stuck with investing in companies I bought from regularly and admired. My first phone (after a flip phone) was an iPhone. I go to Starbucks often and my local store is always packed. I shop from Amazon. Those are three companies right there that I could have invested in early on because I had a lot of first-hand knowledge about them. Of course, I didn't because I chose some other stocks of companies I knew less well.

Fortunately, I have learned some lessons along the way. When you reach the end of this book you'll see how I used the PALMS filtering system to pick one of those companies and buy its stock.

I'm pointing out this advantage because you probably know three companies well, companies just like Amazon, Apple, and Starbucks that I mentioned above. As you read on in this book I hope you'll remember to write them down on your list so you can keep track of them and whether they pass the PALMS filters.

Keep in mind that all of the research, thinking, and analysis of financial statements are not enough to make you a great investor. If it were all you would have to do is spend a lot of time reading and you'd be rich. As the hedge-fund managers proved when they lost the bet with Buffett, all of the analysis, brains, business connections, and financial statement reading do not make a great investor. There are other traits like intuition and understanding companies as a devoted customer that are more important.

Reading financial statements is not everything in investing; it's merely one component. I'll show you how to read annual reports so you can find out if a company is making or losing money.

How to read annual reports

I did not know anything about financial statements when I bought my first stocks, and some of my early investments have delivered great returns that continue to compound in value. These were easy decisions to make — I simply bought shares in great, profitable companies with moats selling at a sensible price. Similarly, you can make intelligent decisions without reading financial reports. However, I do believe that over time you'll be better off when you can develop fluency reading annual reports, and if you're like me, you may even start to enjoy them.

I especially like reading the letter that the CEO writes to shareholders at the beginning of every annual report. These letters and the entire report are free to download and will give you a good feel for the company. I like to read Jeff Bezos' letter to Amazon shareholders and I think you'll also find it a good shareholder letter to start with. Also, check out Warren Buffett's letter to Berkshire Hathaway shareholders and the annual reports of any company that interests you. You can just Google for the annual report and read it minutes later.

Keep in mind that profitability is just one facet of investing, and financial reports are simply one tool to use. As you read this chapter, I hope you will not be too hard on yourself if you don't grasp every detail right away. If you are not an accountant or professional investor then you will not have spent much time studying this "foreign language" of accounting, and like any new language, it will take time to become fluent. I encourage you to read through and just try to get a good understanding of the key things to look at, which you will learn in this chapter. They will help you understand the annual reports you read in the future.

To determine profitability, you will need to learn to read an income statement. It's very easy to do, and I'm going to show you how. You will also benefit from learning to read a balance sheet, which shows you a company's financial health. I will show you how to read both types of financial statements in this chapter. You first need to view the company's financial statements.

Downloading a company's annual report

You can locate and download any publicly-traded company's annual report by visiting the company's website, and then go to the "Investor Relations" section of their website. Then download the annual report (it's a free download, usually in PDF form). Go to the "Financials" section where you will find the "Income Statement" and also the "Balance Sheet."

Screenshot of The Walt Disney Company's investor relations page. All publicly-traded companies have investor relations pages on their websites. You can order an annual report and have it mailed to you, or you can download it from the website. To download the annual report from the website, just click the "INVESTOR RELATIONS" navigation tab on the top row.

1. Do an Internet search for the company name followed by the words "annual report."
2. Click on the "Investor Relations" tab.
3. Locate the "Annual Report" link and click that.
4. Once you have downloaded the annual report, read the "Letter to Shareholders" to get an overview of the company.
5. Flip through the annual report until you get to Form 10-K which contains the financial statements. You want to find the "Income Statement," which provides information about the company's profitability.

Income statements show a business's revenue, expenses, and income.

The income statement shows all of a business's income and expenses over the most recent quarter and past few years. Look for the line at the bottom of the page that says "Net Income." If it has parentheses around it that is a loss. That means the company is unprofitable. If the number has no parentheses then the company is profitable. See the screenshots on the next page for clear examples.

The income statement from Tesla that you'll see in the next pages covers the period from 2013 until 2016. As you will see, the company has lost money every year. Tesla has a chance to dominate the electric vehicle market and become a leader in autonomous driving technology, but there is no guarantee this will happen, or that it will happen as management hopes. Tesla may not make enough vehicles to sell them at a fast enough rate to become profitable for many years. You are taking a risk if you buy Tesla stock that their plans may not come to fruition, and if you buy the stock at too high a price and it falls considerably, there is a real chance you may never see the stock price return to your purchase price.

There is nothing inherently wrong with speculating in a company like Tesla, and some speculation can be healthy. I just want you to be clear when you are investing and when you are speculating, and if you're starting I think it makes more sense to stick with investing in companies that are already turning a profit.

Look at the line that says "Net Income," which is another way of saying "profits." A glance at Tesla's income statement will reveal dollar amounts in parentheses, which indicate losses. In other words, Tesla has never been profitable.

This book encourages you to invest only in profitable companies, and Tesla does not currently fit the bill. This does not mean it will not be profitable in the future; it might one day be enormously successful. Currently Tesla stock does not appear to be a strong candidate to compound investment returns with low risk of losing money; it represents a speculative venture and not an investment. Let's take a look at Tesla's income statement.

Annual Income Statement (values in 000's)					Get Quarterly Data	
Period Ending:	Trend	12/31/2016	12/31/2015	12/31/2014	12/31/2013	
Total Revenue		$7,000,132	$4,046,025	$3,198,356	$2,013,496	
Cost of Revenue		$5,400,875	$3,122,522	$2,316,685	$1,557,234	
Gross Profit		$1,599,257	$923,503	$881,671	$456,262	
Operating Expenses						
Research and Development		$834,408	$717,900	$464,700	$231,976	
Sales, General and Admin.		$1,432,189	$922,232	$603,660	$285,569	
Non-Recurring Items		$0	$0	$0	$0	
Other Operating Items		$0	$0	$0	$0	
Operating Income		($667,340)	($716,629)	($186,689)	($61,283)	
Add'l income/expense items		$119,802	($40,144)	$2,939	$22,791	
Earnings Before Interest and Tax		($547,538)	($756,773)	($183,750)	($38,492)	
Interest Expense		$198,810	$118,851	$100,886	$32,934	
Earnings Before Tax		($746,348)	($875,624)	($284,636)	($71,426)	
Income Tax		$26,698	$13,039	$9,404	$2,588	
Minority Interest		$98,132	$0	$0	$0	
Equity Earnings/Loss Unconsolidated Subsidiary		$0	$0	$0	$0	
Net Income-Cont. Operations		($674,914)	($888,663)	($294,040)	($74,014)	
Net Income		($674,914)	($888,663)	($294,040)	($74,014)	
Net Income Applicable to Common Shareholders		($674,914)	($888,663)	($294,040)	($74,014)	

Tesla's income statement. See the "Net Income" line which shows profits. The parentheses around the net income figures show that Tesla has been unprofitable every year of its existence.

When reading an income statement, any numbers within parentheses indicate losses. Tesla has never been profitable, and this is often the case with companies in "start-up" mode who have yet to earn more money than they pay in expenses. Many start-ups reinvest earnings into growing the company and because of this, it can take many years for a new company to show a profit.

While it's not bad for a company to be unprofitable, for the sake of this book I want to encourage you to focus on companies that have demonstrated the ability to be profitable. This way you don't have to risk investing in a company that may never turn a profit.

Tesla stock may be worth considering in the future, especially if the company can produce electric cars and sell them at a profit. When this happens Tesla stock may make sense as an intelligent investment. Just keep in mind for now that if you want to invest in a company like Tesla, you are hoping the company will become profitable. That is gambling, and it's different from investing, where you already know the company is profitable.

You don't ever want to confuse gambling with investing — either in your thinking or in your investing account. If you ever decide you want to invest in a company that is not profitable, and it's a speculation, I recommend doing so in a separate account, so you keep speculation apart from investing in your mind, and also in your accounts.

On the following pages let's look at Lowes and Disney as examples of profitable companies. While there is a lot you can learn about financial statements in the future, all you need to do now is focus on the "Net Income" line at the bottom. If you see it's a positive number the company is profitable. Let's take a look at Lowes' income statement.

Annual Income Statement (values in 000's)					Get Quarterly Data
Period Ending:	Trend	2/3/2017	1/29/2016	1/30/2015	1/31/2014
Total Revenue	▮▮▮▮	$65,017,000	$59,074,000	$56,223,000	$53,417,000
Cost of Revenue	▮▮▮▮	$42,553,000	$38,504,000	$36,665,000	$34,941,000
Gross Profit	▮▮▮▮	$22,464,000	$20,570,000	$19,558,000	$18,476,000
Operating Expenses					
Research and Development	------	$0	$0	$0	$0
Sales, General and Admin.	▮▮▮▮	$15,129,000	$14,105,000	$13,272,000	$12,865,000
Non-Recurring Items	------	$0	$0	$0	$0
Other Operating Items	▮▮▮▮	$1,489,000	$1,494,000	$1,494,000	$1,462,000
Operating Income	▮▮▮▮	$5,846,000	$4,971,000	$4,792,000	$4,149,000
Add'l income/expense items	------	$0	$0	$0	$0
Earnings Before Interest and Tax	▮▮▮▮	$5,201,000	$4,419,000	$4,276,000	$3,673,000
Interest Expense	------	$0	$0	$0	$0
Earnings Before Tax	▮▮▮▮	$5,201,000	$4,419,000	$4,276,000	$3,673,000
Income Tax	▮▮▮▮	$2,108,000	$1,873,000	$1,578,000	$1,387,000
Minority Interest	------	$0	$0	$0	$0
Equity Earnings/Loss Unconsolidated Subsidiary	------	$0	$0	$0	$0
Net Income-Cont. Operations	▮▮▮▮	$3,093,000	$2,546,000	$2,698,000	$2,286,000
Net Income	▮▮▮▮	$3,093,000	$2,546,000	$2,698,000	$2,286,000
Net Income Applicable to Common Shareholders	▮▮▮▮	$3,093,000	$2,546,000	$2,698,000	$2,286,000

Lowes' income statement. By looking at the line that says "Net Income" you can see that Lowes' has steadily increased its profits.

Look at the "Net Income" line and you will see a gradual progression in net income (profits) for Lowes. This income statement shows that Lowes has generated steadily increasing profits. Let's take a look at Disney's income statement.

Annual Income Statement (values in 000's)					Get Quarterly Data
Period Ending:	Trend	9/30/2017	10/1/2016	10/3/2015	9/27/2014
Total Revenue		$55,137,000	$55,632,000	$52,465,000	$48,813,000
Cost of Revenue		$30,306,000	$29,993,000	$28,364,000	$26,420,000
Gross Profit		$24,831,000	$25,639,000	$24,101,000	$22,393,000
Operating Expenses					
Research and Development		$0	$0	$0	$0
Sales, General and Admin.		$8,176,000	$8,754,000	$8,523,000	$8,565,000
Non-Recurring Items		$98,000	$156,000	$53,000	$140,000
Other Operating Items		$2,782,000	$2,527,000	$2,354,000	$2,288,000
Operating Income		$13,775,000	$14,202,000	$13,171,000	$11,400,000
Add'l income/expense items		$78,000	$0	$0	($31,000)
Earnings Before Interest and Tax		$14,173,000	$15,128,000	$13,985,000	$12,246,000
Interest Expense		$385,000	$260,000	$117,000	$0
Earnings Before Tax		$13,788,000	$14,868,000	$13,868,000	$12,246,000
Income Tax		$4,422,000	$5,078,000	$5,016,000	$4,242,000
Minority Interest		($386,000)	($399,000)	($470,000)	($503,000)
Equity Earnings/Loss Unconsolidated Subsidiary		$320,000	$926,000	$814,000	$854,000
Net Income-Cont. Operations		$9,300,000	$10,317,000	$9,196,000	$8,355,000
Net Income		$8,980,000	$9,391,000	$8,382,000	$7,501,000
Net Income Applicable to Common Shareholders		$8,980,000	$9,391,000	$8,382,000	$7,501,000

Disney's income statement. If you look at the "Net Income" line you can see the gradual increase in profits from 2014 through 2017. Disney has steadily increased profits although profits for 2017 were not as great as the prior year's profits.

Profitability is a good first hurdle for any company you're considering for investment. If you stick to companies that prove they can make money over time you will be on the right track to growing your investment over time. Buying stock in companies that you hope will become profitable is a risky bet.

I think there is a big temptation to buy companies that have exciting technology. New things are inherently cool and I think investors like owning stock of the next new thing. People buy shares of Tesla, Snapchat, and many other companies that have exciting potential futures, but without profits, all they need is bad news for the company or economy to seriously harm its future earnings potential and cause the stock price to fall quickly and unexpectedly.

In summary, the only things a company can offer shareholders are either the promise of future earnings (profits), share buybacks at sensible prices, or the distribution of dividends to shareholders.

If there is a lot of uncertainty about whether a company will become profitable, then it's a gamble. If a company has already proven profitability, then uncertainty decreases, and instead of gambling one is investing.

A FOR ADAPTABLE

Is this company ADAPTING to Technology?

As you think about a stock ask yourself if the company is adapting quickly to technology in a way that helps customers. If they are then you may be onto something. Read customer reviews, check out the company's app in the Apple Store or Google Play, and see if customers give it high marks. You want to get a pulse of which companies are really "getting it" and evolving with the times to serve customers well. If a company you are considering is leading the way by rapidly adapting to new technologies and providing services and products that attract customers, then its stock is worthy of further consideration.

Let me share the example of Progressive Insurance, the car insurance company. I recently learned that Progressive uses technology to monitor its customers' driving habits so it can offer safe driving discounts. Now, if you put the "Big Brother" issue aside — I'm not so sure I'd want my driving monitored by my insurance company — the company might be providing something useful to customers.

If Progressive tells a customer they can save $150 if they'll allow tracking of the speed they drive, etc, that might be a competitive advantage for the company. Suddenly they can segment their customers into those that are low-risk for accidents and give them a discount. Not all customers will want this, but those that do can save more money. In this way, technology can help the company gain loyal customers.

I'm not an expert on Progressive or car insurance, but it seems the company is leading the way as an insurer by adapting to new technology in a way that can potentially help customers. If you look for companies that are on the leading edge like that it will help you figure out ahead of time which companies might be gaining a competitive advantage. I don't own Progressive stock, but I've followed the stock for years. It's one of the stocks I wish I had bought when I first learned about it many years ago!

Today's companies need to adapt quickly to changing technologies or they will perish. Companies in all industries need to adapt to meet consumer demands and stay ahead of the competition.

I'm going to share a few examples of companies that adapt quickly to new technologies. There are hundreds of other companies handling the task well, and I'm just mentioning a few familiar ones to give you an idea of the kinds of companies that are on the leading edge of innovation.

Amazon

Amazon CEO Jeff Bezos decided early on that his company would always innovate on behalf of, and obsess about customers. He believes that it's not the customer's job to tell Amazon what they want, it's Amazon's job to innovate on behalf of customers.

A culture of innovation drives everything that Amazon does, and it's crucial to the "Always Day 1" mantra that Bezos claims is one of the keys to Amazon's success. The company retains the energy and drive to innovate and start-up mentality by always thinking as though the company needs to invent and adapt to customer desires and needs. He said that the goal is for Amazon to never become a "Day 2" company, where people get used to doing things the way they've always been done when people get comfortable or complacent.

One of the keys to Amazon's success is that the company is always thinking of ways to make its products cheaper and deliver them faster. Bezos says that customers will always want faster delivery.

"A customer will never be unhappy because you delivered their order faster than expected," Bezos said. Adapting to consumer needs, and creating new technologies like Amazon's Echo is just one way Amazon innovates new ways to deliver the goods faster and cheaper than its competition.

Square

Square lets small businesses accept credit cards for retail transactions quickly and easily. The company has adapted well to changes in retailing, and this bodes well for its future. Many of its customers use Square registers, and many others use a card reader to let them accept payments on their phones.

An example of Square quickly adapting to technology: when credit cards changed to chip reader technology from swipe technology, Square quickly made chip-readers available. This rapid adaptation of new technology made Square an easy choice for a partner when Starbucks decided it needed a point-of-sale phone payment system in its stores; Square was the natural fit.

By continually innovating to become a useful feature of the retail landscape, Square ensures that it will not easily become irrelevant. The company has even made it possible for small businesses to create invoices on their mobile phone and send them to clients who can then pay the invoice with a credit card. This innovation makes it easy for small businesses to get paid quickly and easily, and it ensures a secure transaction for the buyer as well.

Square's business adapts rapidly to changes in technology. They have consistently improved their apps and website offerings to anticipate the needs of small businesses and improve the retail experience.

Starbucks

Starbucks has adapted to the changing digital world by developing an app that is becoming heavily used by its customers. The Starbucks app lets customers pay for coffee, food, or other store products using the app, and when they purchase they earn "stars" which are part of a loyalty program that rewards regular users with drinks or food when they reach a certain number of stars earned.

The company has recognized the rapid adoption of the app, with more users signing up every year since the app has been in use. Customers can order using the mobile app before they arrive in a cafe, and pick up their orders once they arrive. Mobile ordering has not been without its problems, as some stores have had problems keeping up with the rapid adoption and in-store customers have had to wait as mobile orders are filled, but these bottlenecks have been addressed and with time will likely be fixed.

Companies that integrate technology and make it easy for customers to use their mobile devices will likely do well in the future, while those that are slow to adapt are surely going to be outcompeted by more nimble rivals.

7

L FOR LOYAL

LOYAL customers drive successful brands

L oyalty can't be measured with math. Understanding the loyalty that customers have toward a product or service is an enormous advantage to an investor, and you can use your first-hand knowledge of customer loyalty as your investing edge.

When you go to a favorite store and it's always packed with customers, you witness customer behavior that Wall Street analysts don't see. When you notice that your friends all tend to buy the same kind of phone, or all like to go to the same restaurants or use the same social networks, you see details that give you an edge. You probably already know which businesses have loyal customers and which ones don't.

Wall Street analysts may be good when it comes to numbers, but because they spend so much time analyzing financial data and reading earnings reports that they miss out on useful first-hand information that customers like you possess. Just think, every time you buy things online or visit stores you are learning about companies. You already know a lot about several companies just based on where you spend your money. Your unique retail experiences give you a huge advantage over financial analysts who lack the kind of direct experience you have with the brands you like.

Loyalty is one of those intangible qualities that does not fit neatly into a box in a spreadsheet. Look at the brands you see around you and you'll see a pack of loyal customers who rally around that company every day. When you consider investing in a company, try to see if it has loyal customers. Brand loyalty is powerful because it ensures repeat business.

To invest successfully, you already have an edge — because of your experience as a loyal customer of several brands. For example, a friend of mine has an iPhone, and so do his father and mother. He would not buy any other brand other than an iPhone. Their whole family is loyal to Apple — not only their iPhones but they all own MacBook Pros. I know many families like this, where they own all the latest devices, from iPads to watches. This loyalty to the brand ecosystem ensures the company's success for years to come.

I'm sure this story is familiar to you. Even if you don't have an iPhone, you can see how many people around you choose Apple products without question, and when their devices break they go back to Apple for a replacement, never considering another brand. When you combine loyalty with other factors in the PALMS system you'll start finding profitable companies with consistent sales and a growing base of new customers.

Thinking in terms of brand loyalty gives you an extra tool in your toolkit that many investors don't use. When you combine it with other filters you're starting to use a "multi-pronged" approach to investing. There is a saying, "To a man with a hammer, every problem is a nail." Well, if all you use is math to evaluate companies, then you're at a huge disadvantage when you go up against someone who considers intangible factors like loyalty.

Loyalty is a powerful tool

Understanding customer loyalty is a powerful tool, and it's often over-looked or undervalued when looking at stocks. Those who get distracted by moving ticker symbols and looking at charts can often miss the essential, simple, and powerful results of focusing in on a company with loyal customers.

Loyalty is a powerful, yet hard to define business characteristic. A company with loyal customers spends less money because they don't have to constantly find new customers. Loyal customers are so enthu-siastic that they become a source of free advertising for the brand, and they bring a high level of excitement for a company's products and services that money just can't buy.

I searched Google for "Brands With Most Loyal Customers" and found this list.[1] Brand Keys, the consultancy that conducted the survey, looked at 740 brands to arrive at these 20 companies:

1. Amazon (online retail)
2. Google
3. Apple (tablets)
4. Netflix
5. Apple (smartphones)
6. Amazon (video streaming)

7. Samsung
8. Facebook
9. Amazon (tablets)
10. YouTube
11. Dunkin' Donuts
12. Nike
13. Trader Joe's
14. WhatsApp
15. iTunes
16. Hyundai
17. Starbucks
18. Ford
19. PayPal
20. Domino's

Loyalty is a powerful profit driver for each of these companies, and how customers relate to them. These brands have a place in customers' hearts. You can't learn of these "intangible" qualities by combing through financial statements, but if you are a customer of these (or other) companies, then you probably have some unique understanding about customer loyalty that another investor might not possess.

It makes sense to incorporate customer loyalty into a filtering system. It tells us that customers feel something "emotional" or a "bond" to the brand, and over time this can help a company fend off competition. You can call it stickiness or loyalty or whatever you'd like, but the important "take-home" message is that if you can identify companies with strong loyalty, you are likely to have found a company that will continue to have a stream of revenue from these clients for many years into the future. As you can see, from the list above, Amazon and Apple appear twice on the list for loyalty for different products.

Many companies have loyal followings. I will provide one example below that I know well because of all of my experience as a professional photographer. I use Adobe products (Photoshop and

Lightroom) every day and I also know many photographers. I can say without hesitation that every serious photographer uses Photoshop.

I'll explain why Adobe exemplifies a business with loyal customers. I hope you'll take a moment to ask yourself how if a company that you're considering for investment has loyal customers. One way to define loyal customers is repeat buyers who will be unlikely to switch to a competitor because they have a personal connection with the brand, they feel an almost irrational connection to the products, and they use them reflexively. If the brand name is also a verb, that's a good sign that the company has loyal devotees: think FedEx, Photoshop, etc.

ADOBE SYSTEMS

Adobe makes the best photo editing software system on earth. There are no serious competitors out there. I'm not saying there are not some image editing programs available, but none where the name of the program has become a verb like "Photoshopping."

Photographers, designers, filmmakers, visual artists, and marketers have formed a strong bond with Adobe's products like Photoshop, Illustrator, InDesign, Lightroom, and Premiere. The loyalty is intense; I don't know of a single photographer who doesn't use Photoshop, nor do I know any designers who don't use Illustrator or InDesign regularly.

Adobe has millions of loyal customers for its products and enjoys very little competition because of the "switching cost" of time that users of software like Photoshop, Illustrator, and Premiere would have to spend learning how to use a competitor's products. This "learning hurdle" ensures that Adobe will retain loyal users for years to come.

GEICO

GEICO is a wholly-owned subsidiary of Berkshire Hathaway Corp., and while you can't buy stock in GEICO directly, it's a great example of a company that has loyal customers.[2] The company's overall cost structure is low, and by selling directly to the consumer they avoid having to pay rent for retail locations, etc. Their service is top-notch, which means they retain customers, and this in turn makes for a solid business model because they have frequent renewals, which translates into less money spent trying to retain customers. They simply renew and this process makes keeping customers inexpensive.

Customer loyalty is an enormous part of GEICO's success. They have a large and growing customer base, and these customers spread the world, and gradually the company's market share has grown.

As you search for companies as investments, you would be well served by looking for companies like GEICO that have a low-cost structure, have been growing their market share consistently over time, and have many loyal and happy customers.

NIKE

Nike is one of the great all-time brands and has a loyal following. There's not a lot to be said about the company that people in all countries don't already understand. They started with sneakers and branched out into all kinds of athletic apparel. They have remained relevant over the years to older generations while appealing to the young. I recently had the chance to make friends with a family in my seat row on a flight from San Diego to Seattle, and one of their sons, who was in high school, told me he has a business of buying new Nike sneakers when they are released and reselling them on eBay at a huge markup.

I'm not privy to all of the hype and excitement about the Nike brand, but the company has found a way to appeal to people and make shoes that are not only worn for sports and fashion, but collected as artwork. Nike undoubtedly knows about this attraction (they created the demand for it, after all) and they have found a way to release some sneakers in limited supply so as not to flood the market.

The constant innovation, finger on the pulse of fashion and

sports, and awareness of the importance of scarcity all point to the intelligence of a company that straddles the worlds of art, athletics, and commerce. The way they connect with customers' hearts and minds, as well as their bodies, ensures that the Nike brand will remain relevant for many years to come. As an investor, you want to be on the lookout for companies with many loyal customers; they make repeat business and consistent cash flow more likely, and improve your odds of long-term investment success.

Loyal customers mean repeat business

Loyal customers equal repeat business, which means a company that has loyal customers does not have to keep spending money to retain customers, or constantly find new customers. Recurring streams of income are the lifeblood of a company, and the company with loyal customers has a constant source of fresh cash flowing in every day.

Leaders

Leaders are a very important part of any company that you consider for investment. I have thought that the "L" in the PALMS system could (and an argument could be made that it should) stand for "Leaders" instead of Loyalty.

To be clear, when I talk about leaders I'm talking about the CEO of a company, and in some cases, such as Berkshire Hathaway's, I'm talking about the partnership of Buffett and Munger who together have led the company for decades. Outstanding leadership can be hard to quantify, but it drives a company's success. Think of Bezos' role at Amazon or Jobs at Apple and you can see how having a leader with a clear vision and ability to make a few great decisions each year can be of enormous benefit to a company. Take away that leader and the company floats aimlessly or sinks. Many great companies have been ruined by lousy leaders.

It is hard to tell you how to know what leaders are great and will continue to make intelligent decisions in the future, and which ones will flounder. These things are often apparent after the fact, but if you're not investing in a large company with a well-known CEO then it is very difficult to gauge the talent and integrity of someone you've never met.

For this reason, I choose "Loyal" for the L because we all know about brands with loyal customers, and the brands like Nike, Google, Apple will probably be around in 10, 20, or 30 years (or more) and they will be earning a lot more money in the future than they are now. The leaders will come and go, and some will be good and some will not, and it's a very difficult task for any investor to try and assess the talent of a CEO before investing.

I would say that it makes sense to learn as much as you can about the CEO, to watch some YouTube videos, read articles, and of course, read the company's annual report before you invest. If you agree with the CEO's letter and you believe they understand their industry, the company, and get as good an idea as possible if you think they are talented and capable enough to carry out their plan. This is an almost impossible task (to predict the unpredictable) yet that is why investing is so challenging. If you buy stock in a company that is run by people with high integrity and with loads of talent, everything else will fall into place.

So I stick to my advice of searching for companies with loyal customers who are likely to come back and buy again and again, yet I also want to encourage you to keep your eyes out for the other "L" and look for leaders with high ethical standards and the ability to make a few great decisions each year.

8

M FOR MOAT

A moat provides a durable competitive advantage

Another way to express this advantage is to say that an economic moat makes a business *resistant to competition*. A physical moat is a deep, wide ditch surrounding a castle often filled with water as a defense against attack. Similarly, a business moat is a hard-to-duplicate quality that makes it difficult for competitors to copy a business or take its customers.

You want to invest in companies that widen their economic moats to ensure they survive and thrive. A moat prevents competitors from taking their customers and reducing market share. If you invest in a company without a moat, then any new competitor that comes along can take its customers.

A moat provides protection

An example of a wide moat business would be Coca-Cola. If I gave you $100 million and told you to try and make a cola that could outsell Coke, you couldn't do it. It's been tried many times by many cola companies, but the Coca-Cola brand is too strong in the minds of customers, which provides the company with a wide moat.

Disney is another wide-moat company. They have Mickey Mouse, movies like Star Wars and the Marvel series, Pixar, ABC, ESPN, 12 theme parks and 51 resorts. It would be really hard to knock Disney out of business.

The same could be said of Alphabet, the parent company of Google. More people use Google for search than any other search engine. And more people watch YouTube videos than videos on any other platform. I would say Google has a wide moat because it would be hard to replace it with another search engine. When people want an answer to a question they Google the answer. I think it would be extremely hard to change that behavior, hence the wide moat for Google.

Starbucks has a wide moat because it would be hard to build a network of coffee stores around the world and outcompete Starbucks. They have built a network and a recognizable brand and have economies of scale. That network would be very hard for a large chain to harm. The barriers to entry would be very high, and Starbucks would squash the competition.

McDonald's has a brand that's recognizable all over the world and its size and scale would make it extremely hard for any company to come along and try to displace them as the fast-food leader. There are other companies whose brand names and global reach give them wide moats: Burger King, KFC, Pizza Hut, and Taco Bell are among the most successful wide moat global brands.

In clothing and footwear, Nike also has a wide moat; it would be hard to displace them as the leading sneaker and athletic wear company in the world. Adidas has tried with limited success, and so has Under Armor, but the iconic Nike and its ubiquitous swoosh define the brand and provide a moat that is unparalleled in the athletic footwear and apparel industry.

What are the characteristics of a moat?

According to Warren Buffett, "The ideal moat...obviously...something that would be protected from any competition. Usually, earnings are regulated in businesses like that. The perfect product is something that costs a penny and sells for a dollar and is habit-forming[1].

Speaking of Coke, Buffett said, "In 1886 some guy named John Pemberton down in a pharmacy in Atlanta hit the wrong spigot or something and it came out and every year, pretty much, since then, sales have increased around the world.

"The products you want have a ubiquity to them," he said. "Coca-Cola travels — Sees candy, which we own, does not travel. We can make all kinds of money in California, but if we try to travel east — we were in Bloomingdales and different places, it doesn't travel. Candy bars don't travel very well. I mean, Cadbury doesn't do very well here, and Hershey doesn't do very well over there...Coca Cola travels...it's universal.

"There's [sic] different qualities you're looking at," Buffett said, "but basically you're trying to find something where you think you have a very high probability about being right about predicting the earning power out 5, 10, and 20 years...and that does depend on competitive positions. You don't want to depend too much on great management. I mean, if a business needs great management, you know, it probably isn't much of a business. I really like a business, ideally, that your idiot nephew can run, and then put in a good manager and do way better!"

Examples of companies with wide moats

The following companies exhibit characteristics of an ideal moat. Adobe, Apple, Amazon, Berkshire Hathaway, Boeing, Colgate-Palmolive, Clorox, Costco, Ferrari, Gilead, Google, Facebook, Intuitive Surgical, Mastercard, McDonald's, Medtronic, Microsoft, Moody's, Nike, Sanofi, Starbucks, Texas Instruments, Unilever, Union Pacific, Visa, and Walt Disney Company.

Examples of companies without moats

What's are examples of a few companies that have no moat? The Gap makes clothing, but so do hundreds of other retailers, and customers can easily switch between retailers. Ditto for Urban Outfitters and their Anthropologie brand. They don't have enough of a niche, a single exceptional product, or pricing that gives them a competitive advantage.

The camera maker GoPro is another example of a company with no moat: they make a small action camera, but there are many small camera manufacturers, and with more people having a cellphone camera with them at all times, it's getting harder for GoPro to convince customers to buy their specialty camera. GoPro just recently left the drone business but had to exit recently because of steep competition from DJI and other drone manufacturers. This is because GoPro had no moat; there was nothing about their drone that made it special and kept the competition from taking their customers.

Within the restaurant and fast-food industry many companies that have no moat because customers can easily go to another restaurant whenever they want. Alaska Airlines, Chipotle, Delta Airlines, Dunkin Donuts, Fiat Chrysler, Ford, General Motors, Lululemon, Subway, Tesla and United Airlines, Volkswagen, Wendy's are a few examples. There is no loyalty, no switching costs, intense industry competition, and low barriers to entry that make it challenging for restaurant operators to build an economic moat.

Examples of companies with moats

Do you remember how in Part 1 I discussed how you should only invest in stocks of companies you understand? Well, I thought it would be helpful to readers to see how I draw up a list of companies with moats that I understand well. I detect moats that protect Adobe, Amazon, Berkshire Hathaway, Carmax, Intuitive Surgical, Nike, Starbucks, Walt Disney, and Waters.

1. Adobe - Wide moat
2. Amazon - Wide moat
3. Berkshire Hathaway - Wide moat
4. Carmax - Narrow moat
5. Intuitive Surgical - Wide moat
6. Nike - Wide moat
7. Starbucks - Wide moat
8. Walt Disney - Wide moat
9. Waters Corporation - Wide moat

More companies with moats

As I told you earlier in the book I was a biology major in college, and I *should have a deep circle of competence* that gives me an edge. Yet honestly, with all of my learning about biology and science, I still do not possess a deep understanding of these companies.

These companies develop and sell drugs and devices, and in my experience, there's a revolving door through which CEOs come and go constantly. Though I have a good understanding of science and medicine I am careful not to invest in these companies — many of which have moats — because they are outside of my circle of competence.

Because I don't have deep knowledge of many of these healthcare companies I don't invest in them. They fall into the "too difficult to understand" pile. Saying no to companies when they are outside your circle of competence is a good idea, and you should never be ashamed to admit you don't know everything about every company. Many of these companies have moats, but I don't understand these businesses well.

1. Abbott Labs - Narrow Moat
2. Baxter - Narrow Moat
3. Becton Dickinson - Narrow Moat
4. Boston Scientific - Narrow Moat
5. Cardinal Health - Wide Moat

6. CVS - Narrow Moat
7. Edwards Lifesciences - Narrow Moat
8. Gilead Sciences - Wide Moat
9. Illumina - Narrow Moat
10. Johnson & Johnson - Wide Moat
11. Medtronic - Wide Moat
12. Nike - Wide Moat
13. Pfizer - Wide Moat
14. Roche Holding - Wide Moat
15. Stryker - Wide Moat
16. Walgreen - No Moat
17. Zimmer Biomet - Wide Moat

The question you may have right now is "How do I know if a company has no moat, a narrow moat, or a wide moat?" and that's an excellent question. No "one" answer exists for every company. Instead, moats change over time depending on how well the company grows its competitive advantages.

Here are a few questions you can ask, and in finding the answers you will discover if a moat exists. Can competition come along and drive them out of business? For example, it would be really hard to invent a cola that could outsell Coca-Cola (many have tried) you probably could not.

On the other hand, LaCroix carbonated water, a product of National Beverage Corporation (FIZZ), has been popular for the past several years, outselling most other water brands. Does LaCroix have a moat? I don't think so, it's just water and although it's got a nice variety of flavors, I think any company could make fizzy water and put it in a nice package.

If you stick to considering companies that have wide moats you won't have to worry as much about that company being driven out of business by a savvy competitor. The presence of a moat provides some confidence the company will endure.

9

S FOR SENSIBLE PRICE

Buy a stock at a sensible price

"Never buy a stock immediately after a substantial rise or sell one immediately after a substantial drop."

— BENJAMIN GRAHAM

E verybody wants to buy stocks when they are cheap. For every buyer, there is a seller, and one of those people winds up on a better side of each trade.

Your goal is to shift the odds in your favor, and one way you can do this is by not overpaying when you buy stock. If you pay too much and the stock price drops a lot *it may never recover* to the price you paid.

One good way to keep this from happening is to be disciplined when it comes to deciding how much to pay. In other words, *don't overpay*. Now, this letter of the PALMS system is one of the hard ones to determine with any certainty because no one knows the exact price. You're better off trying to come up with a range of prices that make sense rather than pick one price with precision.

Benjamin Graham discussed the concept of a "margin of safety" when you buy stock. He encouraged investors to calculate what they believe the stock is worth and buy at a discount to this value. For example, if you decide that a stock is worth $100 and you're seeking a 25% margin of safety — to make up for bad luck or bad math — then you should aim to pay $75 or less. The difference between those two dollar amounts is a margin of safety of $25 and provides the buyer with a *sensible price*.

You want to avoid the mistake of paying too much. One way to do this is not to pile into a stock because everyone else is buying it. If you're buying at an all-time high you're likely paying too much. Sometimes you have to be patient and wait for the market to serve you a sensible price.

Waiting for a sensible price

Sometimes you can screw up if you wait too long for your sensible price. You can make the mistake of not buying a stock that was selling at a fair price because you waited for the perfect price (a low price) that never arrived.

My biggest mistakes have been errors of "omission" rather than errors of "commission." I have lived in Seattle for 20 years, and I've seen companies like Amazon, Microsoft, and Starbucks rise to prominence before my eyes. Microsoft had already become a large and successful company when I arrived in Seattle, but Amazon was just a twinkle in Jeff Bezos' eye when I arrived in Seattle. It turns out he and I took road trips from the east coast (he drove from New York, and I drove from Boston) in 1994. I was moving to Seattle to start my career as a professional photographer, and Amazon had not yet sold its first book.

So, I got to see the Amazon story unfolded before my eyes. It was not always obvious that Amazon would dominate so many industries and have so much success in both retailing and cloud computing.

Many people who worked at Amazon could see that something special was happening at the company, but many outside observers saw another Internet company struggling to turn a profit. Even in the early 2000s, many people thought Amazon might never turn a profit. Yet a lot changed in the next decade or two. One of the most fundamental changes was the small experiment of Amazon Web Services (AWS)[1], which has become wildly successful for Amazon.

AWS got an enormous head start on its competition while building its cloud computing platform in plain sight while competitors like Google, Microsoft, and Oracle sat around and did nothing. Yet, by 2015 it was becoming apparent that something remarkable was happening as Amazon was not only dominating online retailing, but Amazon had become a powerful force in cloud computing.

I noticed that more people had become members of its "Prime" loyalty program that offers expedited shipping, and they bought things from Amazon all the time. I had been a Prime member for years, and I noticed that I was relying on Amazon for lots of purchases.

The Amazon stock price was trading in the $500 range in 2015 and the stock seemed expensive. You have to realize that it had been selling in the $200 range a couple of years earlier. Paying $500 a share seemed like a high price at the time, and I waited around for a lower "entry point" that never materialized. Amazon's stock continued to climb to $600, $700, $800, and then $900 on its way to $1,000. The stock never got cheap.

So, I would say that if you understand a company well, and you're a loyal customer, and you observe that many of your friends or family like buying from the company — don't wait too long to buy the stock.

Sometimes sitting around sucking your thumb and waiting for a lower price can leave you with regret. I think a better approach might be to buy a few shares of stock so you don't miss out altogether. You don't have to invest all of your money right away, but at least you dip your toes in the pool.

The interesting side-effect of buying a small position in a stock is that it causes you to pay more attention because you have "skin in the game" and you'll be more aware of any changes in the company. This will help you stay current and ready to make future investments if the company's prospects remain bright.

Amazon is a rare example of powerful, sustained success that pushes its stock price higher over time without ever getting cheap. Stocks of great companies decline in price every few years, and these opportunities give the patient investor a chance to buy shares at a discount.

These buying opportunities sometimes occur during brief periods, from two or three weeks to a year or more, during which the stock price may decline by 30% - 50%. These are valuable opportunities for the prepared investor who has cash ready to invest.

Patience pays off

I bought my first shares of Berkshire Hathaway about 15 years ago. After that initial purchase, I always wanted to buy more shares, but the company had performed well and the price continued to climb. By 2015 the stock was selling at $140 a share, which I determined to be a fair price. I had money saved to invest in the company, and I wanted to see if I could buy it at a discount.

After waiting for what seemed like an eternity, in January of 2016 I finally got my chance because stock markets started to fall because of economic fears. One day I noticed that the share price for Berkshire "B" shares fell to $125 a share so I went ahead and bought more shares. I just waited a few years for a momentary dip in the stock market and my patience paid off.

I believe that Benjamin Graham's advice to never buy after a substantial rise generally makes a lot of sense. However, with stocks of growing companies like Amazon, which has been growing at a torrid pace for many years, waiting around for a sensible price can prevent you from buying the stock.

You can steer clear of the mistake of paying too much by noting

Graham's warning not to buy a stock right after a substantial rise in price. Sometimes you need to be patient and wait for a sensible price.

The second part of Graham's advice — not selling after a substantial drop — is much easier to do, in my opinion. It doesn't require you to wait for a low price. All you have to do is resist the urge to sell when the market declines. This is easy for me because I not only resist the urge to sell, I'm waiting to buy more shares when they get cheap. As Buffett says, "Be fearful when others are greedy, and greedy when others are fearful."

How to determine a sensible price

I'd like to show you a simple way of determining the sensible price to pay for a stock.

There are a few steps involved because I wanted to break this down into small actionable items. There is some math included as well, but don't be scared off by it. It's not complicated, there are no formulas to memorize.

For this example, let's use the Disney Corporation. Through my initial research, I learned that Disney owns:

- Mickey Mouse
- Frozen
- Star Wars
- Marvel
- Pixar
- ABC
- ESPN

Also, Disney owns 12 Theme Parks, 51 Resorts, 387 stores, has 195,000 employees and $55 billion in revenues.[2]

After all of my reading (annual reports, news articles) to gain a better understanding of the different businesses that Disney owns, I decided that I'd pay $220 billion for the entire Disney company if it were for sale.

1. You need to determine a "sensible price" per share for the company you're considering for investment. To do this you need to take a step back and form an opinion about what the whole company is worth — you were a private buyer and buying the company in its entirely[3]. This next piece of advice is important: *Do not look at the company's stock price* before doing this calculation; it may bias your decision.

2. Next, you need to determine the number of outstanding shares, which are the shares available to trade. It's easy to find this number: just do an online search using the company's name and the words "outstanding shares." For my example, I just searched for "Disney Corporation outstanding shares" and found the total listed as 1,490,777,000 shares.

3. Divide the dollar amount from #1 by the outstanding share number from step #2. The math looks like this: $220,000,000,000 / 1,490,777,000 = $147.57 dollars per share. That is the amount you consider a "sensible price" to buy the company on a "per share" basis.

4. Now that you've decided on your own (unbiased by the quoted price) you can take a look at the current price quote for Disney stock, which, as of March 8th, 2019 is $113.81. The company is selling at a price far below what I would pay for the entire business; less than what I deem a "sensible price," the S in the PALMS filter.

5. In the example above, if you bought Disney stock at $113.81 you would be getting a 22.88% discount on a "per share" basis from your estimated value of $147.57. You can refer to this discount as the "margin of safety,[4]" and it protects you from errors in calculating intrinsic value or worse than average luck. A 22.88% discount is a good margin of safety in case you make an error in your math or have worse than average luck.

What if your math is inaccurate?

It may seem like an enormous challenge for you to form an accurate opinion on the value of a company. There are Wall Street analysts who spend 50 hours a week focused on just one company, or a few companies, and their research is detailed. That does not mean that they have a deeper understanding of a company than you, but I want you to see that some people devote a lot of time to learning.

It's not easy to pinpoint an exact dollar amount that a company is worth, but I believe it's more realistic to come up with a *range of dollar amounts* that you estimate a company to be worth. For this exercise, you have to start with a number, so you can just pick a dollar amount somewhere in the middle of your range. It will help you to get started.

You might be wondering at this point, what if your calculations above were not accurate? What if the company is not worth as much as you thought? Well, you will have *a margin of safety*, and as long as it exists, you can make sure you are not paying a lot more than the quoted price. To be specific, if the company was actually worth $190 billion (and you mistakenly calculated it was worth $220 billion) the actual "sensible price" per share would be:

$190,000,000,000 (actual company value) / 1,490,777,000 (outstanding shares) = $127.45/share

The current price quote of $113.81 for Disney Stock (as of March 8, 2019) represents a 10.71% discount from $127.45, so even if the intrinsic value of the company is $190 billion instead of $220 billion. Buying at $113.81 is less than $127.45 so you are protected in case your math or luck isn't perfect.

According to your estimates of sensible price, you're still getting a discount if you can buy Disney at $113.81. That is the sensible price *you arrived on your own before you checked the stock price.*

Note: The prices above are purely for the sake of the examples, and they don't suggest an opinion about the valuation of Disney or any company mentioned in this book.

Example of a company without a sensible price

There will be times you want to buy a stock, and you're working through the PALMS filter and you've been able to come up with a "yes" for every factor except for the price. I want to give you an example of a company that passes on P, A, L, M, but you get stuck on the S for "Sensible Price."

Let's look at **Costco:**

Profitable: Yes. Costco is profitable. You can check the income statement for proof.

Adaptable: Yes. Costco's model continues to withstand the intensely competitive environment.

Loyal: Yes. Costco has a loyal customer base with strong traffic and 90% US membership renewal rates.

Moat: Yes. Costco has a wide moat that allows Costco to grow market share despite intense competition.

Sensible Price: No. The stock market is currently pricing too much optimism into Costco's shares.

The price is the only factor that keeps Costco from looking like a great investment.

As of March 8, 2019, Costco's stock is currently selling for 227.82/share.[5] In my estimation, a sensible price for these shares is closer to $153/share. There are currently 438,208,000 shares outstanding.

Present Price: $227.82 (current share price) x 438,208,000 (shares outstanding) = $99,832,510,000 total company value

Sensible Price: $153 (if stock price declines) x 438,208,000 (shares outstanding) = $67,045,810,000 total company value

I think an investor would be better off waiting for a lower price which provides a better margin of safety.

As you can see, a decrease in stock price means you're getting the entire company (on a per-share basis) for much less money. There is always the chance that you will never see a lower price for Costco stock, so if you want to buy the stock I would suggest you heed Warren Buffett's advice, "It's far better to buy a wonderful company at a fair price than a fair company at a wonderful price." In my view, Costco is a wonderful company and the price is close to fair (perhaps only a little expensive) so if you plan on holding these shares for 5-10 years then you can always buy some shares now and wait to see if you can get a lower price for future share purchases.

A problem with Wall Street analysts

Many Wall Street analysts are good at analyzing numbers, but they put too much emphasis on financial math. To understand a business well you have to use your knowledge and experience.

If you use your investigative powers rather than rely on the same financial data that analysts consider you will have an edge over those who rely solely on financial statements.

Three tips to avoid buying after the price has gone up a lot

1. Remind yourself that you are investing in a company. "A stock is not just a ticker symbol or an electronic blip; it is an ownership interest in an actual business, with an underlying value that does not depend on its share price." — Ben Graham, "The Intelligent Investor."[6]
2. Ask yourself "Would I be happy owning this company for the next 5 to 10 years?" Only buy if your answer is "yes."
3. Look up the currently quoted price for the stock. Is it at or near a 52-week high? If the answer is "yes," then wait for the price to fall. Try not to buy at the all-time high.

This approach will ensure you don't pay the "highest price" ever for the stock. The problem with this approach is that if the stock price never declines, you may never buy the stock.

Seth Klarman, a respected value investor, explained the benefits of buying a stock at a low price. "We all know that the evidence shows that when you enter at a low price, you will have good returns, and

when you enter at a high valuation, you will have poor returns,"
Klarman said. "Avoiding round trips and short-term devastation
enables you to be around for the long term."[7]

It's good to have stock prices do nothing

Warren Buffett made this observation back in 1963:

*"...Our business is one requiring patience. It has little in common with a
portfolio of high-flying glamour stocks...It is to our advantage to have securities do nothing price-wise for months, or perhaps years, while we are
buying them. This points up the need to measure our results over an
adequate period of time. We suggest three years as a minimum..."*

What if you want to buy an expensive stock?

This is a problem for investors who want to buy stocks at low prices;
the stocks of many great companies today have been going up and up
for many years, and to the casual observer it seems that their stock
prices may never go down to a low price. People are very excited
about the future of companies like Amazon, Apple, Facebook,
Google, Netflix, and others, and they are all piling into these stocks,
paying more and more to own them and in the process, driving the
prices even higher.

Just because others are buying stocks does not mean you should
too. Try to separate your desire to own part of a company from your
fear of missing out on buying hot stocks.

---

*"The line separating investment and speculation, which is never
bright and clear, becomes blurred still further when most market
participants have recently enjoyed triumphs. Nothing sedates
rationality like large doses of effortless money. After a heady
experience of that kind, normally sensible people drift into behavior
akin to that of Cinderella at the ball. They know that overstaying the
festivities — that is, continuing to speculate in companies that have*

gigantic valuations relative to the cash they are likely to generate in the future — will eventually bring on pumpkins and mice. But they nevertheless hate to miss a single minute of what is one helluva party. Therefore, the giddy participants all plan to leave just seconds before midnight. There's a problem, though: They are dancing in a room in which the clocks have no hands."

— BERKSHIRE HATHAWAY 2000 LETTER TO SHAREHOLDERS

So you have a few choices here: you can avoid completely any investment where the price may be too high and steer clear of speculation. Benjamin Graham offers a solution for instances when you want to buy stock, but the price suggests you may be speculating rather than paying a sensible price.

Benjamin Graham's Solution

If the price for a stock you want to buy seems a little too high — it's beyond what you deem sensible, can you "bend the rules" or add flexibility to your filtering system?

I say yes, you can do it, but you should be aware you are doing it. Say to yourself, "I think this stock is more expensive than a sensible investor would pay, and as a way to own a share of this company, I'm speculating a bit." This seems to be a sound approach to intelligent speculation. It lets you invest at a slightly higher price than you'd ordinarily pay without the risk that you'll make a mistake of omission and regret never getting a low enough entry price to buy the stock.

"Speculation is always fascinating, and it can be a lot of fun while you are ahead of the game. If you want to try your luck at it, put aside a portion – the smaller the better – of your capital in a separate fund for this purpose. Never add more money to this account just because the market has gone up and profits are rolling in. Never

mingle your speculative and investment operations in the same account, nor in any part of your thinking."

— BENJAMIN GRAHAM

Graham does not say you can't speculate, but rather he says you must be intentional about it. Don't confuse it in your mind or try to convince yourself that you are investing when in reality you are speculating.

By giving yourself price flexibility on the price you pay, you get the chance to buy shares of a fast-growing company, whereas if you waited for a price decline you may never buy it. As added insurance against paying too high a price, you can always start with a small initial investment, and if the price declines subsequently you can buy more shares.

Final thoughts about paying a sensible price

Investing is an art that requires creative thinking and imagination.

If math skills ensured investing success, then mathematicians could easily become rich.

Having good math skills and applying them to reading financial reports will not make you a good investor. Math and numbers are only one tool — and a small one at that, when it comes to investing. Some of the best investments are made with just a simple understanding and a story you can tell about a company in a few sentences.

This is why the PALMS filtering system is a useful tool; it provides a multidisciplinary framework that requires some qualitative decision-making that you simply can't do with math alone. When you combine several different factors — profitability, adaptability, loyalty, moat, and sensible price — you get a more robust mosaic of the company that lends to your "seeing" a more complete picture.

Each of the PALMS filters requires research and reflection, and your ability to keep track of different items in your head and thoughtfully assemble them to tell a story about the company will become a creative process. No two people understand a company in the same way.

At the end of the day, a company may pass every filter except the sensible price. If you believe the company makes sense on all other criteria except price, considering "paying up" for quality. You may pay more than you want initially, but if it's a great company and you hold for the long term, your investment could appreciate 100%, 300%, 500%, or more.

If you feel confident in every other part of your reasoning, you may want to go ahead and buy a stock that seems expensive. You can always start by buying a small amount, and add more later. This way you will avoid mistakes of omission (you wait for years and never buy as the company grows and the stock price goes up. You can minimize your regret by buying stock in a company, even if it seems a bit expensive. Great companies are seldom cheap because other investors recognize their potential, and, like you, are willing to pay a premium for them.

Stocks won't be expensive all the time. If you wait, there are market dislocations every 5 years or so. To the patient investor, this can provide opportunities. Earlier in this book, we learned how Ted Williams waited for the right pitch. In the same way, a successful investor waits for the right stock at the right price. As Warren Buffett said:

"What's nice about investing is you don't have to swing at every pitch. You can watch pitches come in one inch above or one inch below your navel, and you don't have to swing. No umpire is going to call you out." You get in trouble, Buffett says, when you listen to the crowd chanting "Swing, batter, swing!"[8]

Finally, you must have confidence in your facts and your reasoning. As Benjamin Graham said:

"You're neither right nor wrong because other people agree with you. You're right because your facts are right and your reasoning is right—and that's the only thing that makes you right. And if your facts and reasoning are right, you don't have to worry about anybody else."

A final thought about paying a sensible price. You must be patient because just because you want to invest right now, it doesn't mean that prices are sensible (or cheap). At the time of this writing, stocks have been going up in price for the past 10 years without a serious drop in prices. I would say that it's highly likely that while prices are not entirely overpriced, they are not cheap either.

Keep in mind that super successful investors like Warren Buffett and Charlie Munger, and many others became rich because they were investing at times when many stocks sold at extreme discounts. Stocks went nowhere between 1966 and 1982, even though those times were volatile. Many smart investors took advantage of these very low prices for stocks and bought heavily then. Those low purchase prices are what contributed to their phenomenal returns in the decades that followed.

At the time of this writing, stocks are not selling at low prices by any stretch of the imagination. There are few parts of the market, perhaps with a few exceptions, that anyone could say are sensibly priced. However, for the patient investor, there will be opportunities to buy stocks when markets become irrational and investors are fearful. It's impossible to predict when this will happen, but those who buy stocks when they eventually become cheap will be the investors who get rich when stocks eventually recover.

10

USE YOUR OWN PALMS FILTER

In earlier chapters, you've already written down a list of companies you understand. We've gone through the process of asking the five questions about each company, but I want to make sure it's easy for you to put this to work.

Now that you narrowed the field to companies you understand well for each of them ask yourself these questions:

1. Is the company **P**rofitable?
2. Is the company **A**daptable to technological change?
3. Does the company have **L**oyal customers?
4. Does the company have a **M**oat to protect it from the competition?
5. Is the company stock selling for a **S**ensible price?

If you need a refresher on deciding if a company meets these criteria, just flip back to the start of this chapter. Go through and ask yourself questions. Get curious. Don't be frustrated if you don't have an answer, it just means you need to be patient and learn more.

If anything is too difficult to understand or any question too difficult to answer, don't be afraid to toss it into the "Too Hard" pile and move on to something easier. Remember, you don't get extra points for investing in difficult situations. You get rewarded when the company performs well, and each of these steps in the PALMS filtering system stacks the odds in your favor.

PART III

STICK TO WHAT YOU KNOW

11

A NEW WAY

Investing in the Tech Age

Today's tech stocks are much faster growing with less predictable prospects than the companies that were popular when *The Intelligent Investor*[1] was written — before the age of the Internet. You can learn a lot from that book, but if you rely on it you may find yourself at a huge disadvantage when it comes to assessing companies like Amazon, Alphabet, Apple, Tesla, and Nvidia, among other companies. I learned a lot from Benjamin Graham and highly recommend his book, but I believe that today's investors must update their tool kits to invest in modern times.

Nothing like Amazon, Apple, Facebook, Google, Microsoft, Netflix, Nvidia, Starbucks, Tesla, or Visa existed back in the 1930s, 40s or 50s when Ben Graham invested. It was much easier determine a company's assets, cash flows, and profits and make a reasonable estimate of a fair price to pay for stock because companies and technologies didn't change as quickly as they do today.

I have read the best investing books available. I pulled out some good "time tested" lessons, but I always felt I was missing out because the companies mentioned were so old and not relevant in today's tech-dominated world.

The examples used in those early books were companies like railroads, oil companies, agricultural companies, department stores, electric and gas utilities, telephone, and tobacco companies.

These books had no examples of computer hardware, software, Internet, cloud computing, streaming video, electric cars or tech stocks because these businesses did not exist.

So, while I feel an investor can benefit from the wisdom and lessons that apply to investing in any century, I felt lost without examples that apply to investing in modern times. Today's investors deserve a book that teaches them how to apply the wisdom of the past to today's stocks.

Since no book like this existed yet, I decided to write it myself. The book you hold in your hands is different from many of the books you'll find about the stock market that teach short-term trading, technical analysis, portfolio theory, how to read stock charts, and how to predict short-term stock price movements. These highly speculative tools are not likely to work with any consistency, and they are extremely difficult for investors to master.

Combining great ideas with flexibility

I wrote this book for you, the modern investor, who wants to buy stocks in today's fast-growing companies. This book combines the fundamental wisdom of "old school" investors with a forward-thinking approach that helps an investor make high-velocity decisions to keep pace with rapidly changing companies in the stock market today.

My aim in writing this book is to show a new way to invest; one that retains the best ideas of investors like Warren Buffett, Benjamin Graham, Peter Lynch, and Charlie Munger, and provides new criteria to help investors make fast, high-quality decisions about fast-growing companies. Graham lived before the Internet existed, and Buffett has admitted that he does not have an understanding of technology that he would require to invest in tech stocks.

The founding fathers of investing never knew about the Internet. If you only learn from people who became good investors during an earlier age you won't have the tools necessary to evaluate today's fast-growing cloud computing, Internet and technology companies.

Consider index funds or ETFs

There is something I need to share with you before you dive in and learn about the details of the system that I outline in this book. It's very hard to beat the market and most people won't. Those who do beat the market have a hard time outperforming over long periods.

Anyone can beat the market with a few hot stocks for several months or a year, but continuing to beat the market is difficult. I'm well aware that for many people, picking stocks provides a sense of excitement similar to gambling. There's nothing wrong with feeling those emotions, but you should make sure they don't cause you to make bad decisions.

Index funds and index exchange-traded funds (ETFs) make sense for investors who don't want to spend time researching stocks. While this book educates active investors, readers should be aware that index funds and ETFs are effective ways to capture the market's return.

One approach is to build a solid investing foundation with diversified index funds or ETFs. For example, a total stock market index fund or an S&P 500 index fund provides investors with a diversified portfolio. Once you have invested in the index fund for a while, you can always add stock investments later.

I started with mutual funds when I started investing. I was in my 20s and I didn't know anything about investing in stocks at the time. As I learned more I made a few stock investments, and this was easy to do knowing I already had a solid investing foundation upon which to build.

12

HOW TO INVEST TODAY

Tech Companies Dominate

Companies like Adobe, Alphabet, Amazon, Apple Facebook, Google, Microsoft, Netflix, Nvidia, Tesla, and other fast-growers are the big thing in today's markets. The investing climate is different now than it was just a few years ago.

Some of the great investing books I grew reading — *The Intelligent Investor, Margin of Safety, Common Stocks for Uncommon Profits,* and *One Up on Wall Street*[1] were all great books in their time. Yet if you read them today you won't find mention of the Internet, websites, electric vehicles, the gig economy, or cloud computing. These books were written by investors who had yet to learn of the technological forces that shape our modern world.

I wrote this book because nothing like it exists. There are old books that teach about investing in old-school retail stocks, industrial stocks, and other "brick-and-mortar" businesses, and there are new books that supposedly teach you how to make money easily with day trading, swing trading, and other schemes that make it seem as though anyone can invest easily with little understanding of stocks.

Yes, this book aims to take the investing concepts of the past and apply them to our new tech-dominated world. Investors want to know how to assess stocks of companies in the business of selling electric cars, mobile phones, streaming movies, computers, pet food, exercise bikes, meatless meat, Internet sales platforms, and cloud computing.

We live in an age of rapid innovation, and while companies have changed in the past 100 years, the books about how to invest in companies have not. Ben Graham's seminal book, *The Intelligent Investor*[2], was written in 1949 when a defensive approach to investing made sense to investors, many of whom had the 1929 stock market crash burned freshly in their minds. While it was useful for its time, the modern investor does themself a disservice if they worry about depressions or the last financial crisis or pandemic.

Because of the nature of the tech-dominated economy, and changes to the way the Federal Reserve intervenes during market crises, it is foolish to lean too heavily on the older approaches to assessing companies. Doing so means an investor may miss out on innovative companies like Amazon, Google, Salesforce, Shopify, Tesla, or Zoom. I'm not saying every new tech company that comes along is going to make sense, but I am saying that an investor needs new tools that are useful in the current climate. Readers deserve an intelligent approach to stock picking in the age of technology.

I know you're probably saying, "Sure, I know you think you know a lot about investing, but why should I listen to you when Warren Buffett and other authors have piles of money and long-term records?"

The answer is simple: they developed skill sets that worked during an earlier age. These principles may still work today, but mainly with "old economy" companies because the forefathers of investing did not have expertise in cloud computing, electric cars, graphics processing units, e-commerce, and artificial intelligence. The foundations of our economy have changed enormously, and an intelligent stock investor today needs tools designed for modern times.

This book shows you how to invest in our tech-filled world. It shows you the most important factors to look for when buying a stock, and it shows you a filtering system you can use to quickly and easily evaluate companies and decide if they "make sense" as investments.

Warren Buffett himself recognized the need to adapt, but instead learning about new technologies himself *he hired two bright and energetic investors* who both have fantastic records managing money and constantly read about current businesses, many of which are tech-based.

To address the need to understand investments in technology and other modern businesses, Buffett hired Todd Combs as an investment manager in 2010, and the next year he hired Ted Weschler. At the time, Buffett gave each manager between $1 billion and $3 billion to invest in Berkshire Hathaway's portfolio. With each subsequent year, Buffett has increased the amount of money that each invests, and in the 2017 Berkshire Hathaway Annual Report, Buffett explained that Combs and Weschler, "Each, *independently of me*, manages more than $12 billion; I usually learn about decisions they have made by looking at monthly portfolio summaries."

A few years after Combs and Weschler joined Berkshire, the company made its first investment in Apple Computer. By hiring two new investment managers Buffett effectively expanded Berkshire Hathaway's investing circle of competence[3] because Buffett himself did not know enough to invest in technology and computers. Buffett could have tried moving beyond his circle of competence to learn about Amazon, Apple, or Alphabet, but he did not need to because his new hires understood these businesses better than he did.

This book is geared toward the investor who wants to invest in this modern age. Though you can't hire your own personal Todd Combs or Ted Weschler, *you can use what you already know* to make intelligent decisions. To get started, let's take a look at Google and Amazon, two tech-related companies that confound traditional investors.

Google earns $10 a click

You need to become good at recognizing business models and making decisions when you only have 70% of the information you wish they had. We will go into further depth on this later in the book, but the take-home lesson is that if you have a deep understanding of the company, especially as a customer, then you are in a better position to make an informed investment decision than someone who is not.

For example, if you look at a company like Alphabet (which owns Google), you'll see that they earn money for every ad clicked. Google is not a capital-intensive business, meaning it does not have to continually buy new trucks, maintain airplanes or railroad tracks. They have low capital costs, they hire bright people, and they update their servers and computing equipment. Yet they make money every time someone clicks an ad. Their business is like a toll on the digital highway; a high profit business that costs little to operate and generates cash 24 hours a day.

Alphabet also owns YouTube, which is an enormous profit-generating engine. More people watch videos on YouTube than any other video platform. The company profits every time a viewer watches the ads that play during its videos, and they also profit when people buy its premium "YouTube Red" service to watch ad-free videos. People are watching YouTube videos 24 hours a day around the world.

An investor who sees this continual stream of cash that Google and YouTube generate can make an informed decision on buying Google stock. The earlier an investor can see the value, the better off they'll be compared to other investors who don't see the value or are slow to act. Some investors do not buy tech-related stocks because they don't understand them well enough. The choice today is simple: learn enough to make high quality, quick decisions based on limited information, or do nothing and regret not making a decision when you had a clear picture of what was happening but did not buy stock.

For example, Warren Buffett has never bought Google stock for his company's stock portfolio, and that's something he regrets.[4] At the

2017 Berkshire Hathaway annual shareholders meeting, he told investors he made a mistake by not purchasing shares in the tech giant years ago when Google was earning $10 per click from Geico — a wholly-owned subsidiary of Berkshire.

Buffett said he should have realized Google's enormous profit potential because Geico paid so much for Google Ads. This is not a weakness of Buffett's — he recognizes that Google is beyond the realm of what he understands well — but an investor who does understand some of today's immensely successful companies (many of which are tech-based) will likely do well if they can be decisive a few times in their lifetimes and hold onto the stocks they buy for the long haul.

Don't miss big time

You can miss out on a great stock if you're not flexible enough. You want to have a solid framework for making investment decisions, but realize that businesses change faster today than they did 10 or 20 years ago. I'm not suggesting that you invest in a company you do not understand, or pay an absurdly high price for the stock of a company you do understand, but sometimes you have to act with incomplete information.

Amazon founder & CEO Jeff Bezos said, "Most decisions should probably be made with somewhere around 70% of the information you wish you had.[5] If you wait for 90%, in most cases, you're probably being slow. Plus, either way, you need to be good at quickly recognizing and correcting bad decisions. If you're good at course correcting, being wrong may be less costly than you think, whereas being slow is going to be expensive for sure."

One key to Warren Buffett's investment success is that his first rule of investing is to never lose money, and one way he does this is by being careful not to overpay. His approach works well for him, and to execute on that plan he limits himself to a small group of investments where he has expertise.

Buffett says he missed out by not buying Amazon's stock. "Obviously, I should have bought it long ago," he said, "because I admired it long ago. But I didn't understand the power of the model as I went along. And the price always seemed to more than reflect the power of the model at that time. So, it's one I missed big time."[6]

Be flexible in your thinking, not influenced by investing dogma. Do as much reading and learning as possible *right now*, and be willing to make decisions quickly when you have enough information. You can always course-correct later if you make a bad decision.

High-velocity decision making

Leaders like Bezos make high-quality, high-velocity decisions within their businesses. I believe that investors in these innovative companies must apply the same approach to assessing their stocks.

In other words, you have to develop a high-quality opinion of a company's stock and make a decision quickly. How quickly is up to you, but if you wait three to five years to buy a fast-growing company you might miss the boat. Therefore, you have to adopt the same decisive attitude and ability to decide with "just enough information" in the same way that the companies in which you invest make decisions.

Who would have known just a few years ago that Amazon would be as successful as it has with its voice-activated assistant, Alexa? It looked as though Apple's Siri or Google's Home would lead in this area, but in the blink of an eye, Amazon made enormous strides with artificial intelligence. It is hard to predict which companies will be winners and losers, and if you wait until you see the whole picture develop before your eyes, it might be too late.

Bezos said that the executive leadership team at Amazon is good at making high-quality decisions, and they keep decision-making velocity high. They know that sometimes they'll make bad decisions, yet many decisions are reversible, two-way doors.[7] Buying stock is a reversible decision, because if you make a mistake you can always sell. If you get good at course correcting, being wrong about buying stock will not be costly, whereas being slow is going to be expensive for sure.

13

WHAT IS A STOCK?

Think like an owner

A stock is a piece of ownership of a company. When you buy stock, you don't just own a little number that blinks green and red and jumps up and down on the screen — you become a *part-owner* of a business.

You'll come across the words "shares" and "equities" in your reading, and they both refer to stocks. Even though they represent the same thing — partial ownership of a company — they have slightly different connotations.

Shares get their name because when you buy stock, you actually "share" in the ownership of a company. Investors are referred to as shareholders.

Equities get their name because all of the shares in the company have equal value; none are more valuable than others; there is "equity" among shares.

How do stock owners benefit?

A stock owner can benefit in several ways:

1. The company reinvests its profits. For example, Amazon has been re-investing profits for years to build out its logistics, warehouses, cloud computing business, etc. Those investments, if made wisely, can increase the company's revenue, which can, in turn, increase the value of its shares.

2. The company distributes dividends to shareholders. For example, Disney, Starbucks, and Nike all pay a portion of their earnings to shareholders in the form of dividends. This is money that you can save, spend, or reinvest to buy more shares of stock.

3. The company can "buy back" shares, which means it spends some of its cash to purchase shares, which reduces the number of shares outstanding. The companies earnings are then spread across fewer shares, which increases the earnings per share. The purchase price matters; companies create value when they buy back their stock when it's cheap, and they can destroy value when they overpay.

4. Investors benefit from buying their shares and having the share price rise so they can sell their shares at a higher price for a gain.

5. An investor can lose some, or all of the value of their stock if the underlying company does not turn a profit, can no longer compete, or it is in a struggling sector of the economy. There is no guarantee when you buy stocks that their value will go up, and many companies go out of business every year. For this reason, it is crucial to do your research before investing. You want to increase your chances of success and limit any events that cause the permanent loss of value.

6. I offer this definition of "stocks" because I've noticed that many beginning investors in stocks know little about them. They know they want the stock price to "go up," but they don't realize they are part owners. Rooting for stocks to go up is like speculation or gambling.

A useful investing mindset

Here's a quote by Warren Buffett that expresses what I believe is the right perspective on stock ownership.[1]

"Charlie and I view the marketable common stocks that Berkshire owns as interests in businesses, not as ticker symbols to be bought or sold based other 'chart' patterns, the 'target' prices of analysts or the opinions of media pundits. Instead, we simply believe that if the businesses of the invests are successful (as we believe most will be) our investments will be successful as well. Sometimes the payoffs to us will be modest; occasionally the cash register will ring loudly. And sometimes I will make expensive mistakes. Overall — and over time — we should get decent results. In America, equity investors have the wind at their back."

— WARREN BUFFETT'S BERKSHIRE HATHAWAY 2017
ANNUAL LETTER TO SHAREHOLDERS

You too will have the wind at your back when you invest as though you are an owner of a company — as though you were buying an apartment building or a farm that generates income every year.

When you think of buying stock as becoming an owner in a business you will be patient and learn as much as possible, and you'll make decisions based on your belief on where the company is going in the long term and not based on what might happen next week or next month.

14

FIND YOUR EDGE

"Your investor's edge is not something you get from Wall Street experts. It's something you already have."

— PETER LYNCH

P eter Lynch captures the essence of investment success: "You can outperform the experts if you use your edge by investing in companies or industries you already understand."

You already have a special understanding because of your work, your education, or your hobbies that give you a deep understanding business or the economy, whether you have expertise with cars, clothing, computers, fashion, phones, photography, science, and technology, or any other part of the economy. Let's run through a list of industries so you can get an idea of those where you have expert knowledge.

Here are seven sectors where you may already have an investing edge.

1. Retail / Fashion / Clothing — You know something about: Lululemon, Nike, Victoria's Secret, Ralph Lauren, Old Navy, Gap, Coach, Banana Republic
2. Computer Hardware / Software / Internet Services —You understand Apple, Microsoft, Samsung, Amazon, Netflix, Google
3. Health Care / Pharmaceutical — You understand Pfizer, Gilead Sciences, Express Scripts, CVS, Sanofi, Glaxo Smith-Kline, Novartis, Roche
4. Photography / Digital Imaging / Animation — You understand Canon, Nikon, Adobe Systems, Panasonic, Sony, Fuji, Pixar, Disney
5. Scientific / Measurement / Lab Equipment — You understand Agilent Technologies, Thermo Fisher Scientific, Waters, PerkinElmer, Mettler Toledo, Illumina
6. Cars / Trucks / Hybrid Vehicles / Electric Cars — You understand Toyota, Fiat-Chrysler, Hyundai, Audi, BMW, General Motors, Mercedes, Volkswagen, Subaru, Chevrolet, Ferrari, Honda, Ford, Tesla
7. Aircraft / Transportation / Logistics — You understand Airbus, United Airlines, Delta, American Airlines, Alaska Airlines, JetBlue, Southwest, Boeing, Embraer, Lockheed, Honeywell, UPS, FedEx

Even if you don't know many of the sectors or companies listed above that alright — as an investor you are rewarded for the depth of your knowledge about a few things rather than a shallow understanding of many.

No one has a deep understanding of all companies; it's impossible to have the time required to go into depth on every publicly-traded company.

Warren Buffett says you don't have to know everything; you just have to be clear about what you know. He talks about the concept of a circle of competence, and he suggests drawing a circle around companies you understand and leaving out everything else.

"You don't have to be an expert on every company or even many. You only have to be able to evaluate companies within your circle of competence. The size of that circle is not very important; knowing its boundaries, however, is vital".[1]

— WARREN BUFFETT

There is no shame to pass on things that don't fit into your circle of competence. If something's beyond what you can easily grasp, just pass on it. Warren Buffett has a metal filing box on his desk with the words "TOO HARD" written on it. He says about 99% of the investment ideas he reviews end up there.

He also notes that being excellent in any pursuit doesn't mean you have to be a genius, nor do you have to be good at everything. Buffett notes that Tom Watson, the founder of IBM, put it this way: "I'm no genius. I'm smart in spots—but I stay around those spots.

So, the freeing idea about developing your own edge is to know that you can improve your investing results if you develop the confidence to "just say no" to investments in stocks of companies you don't understand. In other words, your advantage over other investors is the fact that you don't try to have an opinion about every stock out there.

Charlie Munger expressed this concept eloquently when he said, "It's not a competency if you don't know the edge of it. You are a disaster if you don't know the edge of your competency."[2]

Your job provides your edge

My edge comes from my experience as a photographer. I have used Adobe's software programs like Photoshop and Lightroom for about 20 years. Adobe also sells Illustrator, InDesign, Premiere, and many other programs that designers, illustrators, photographers, filmmakers, and marketers use every day all over the world.

Because I use Adobe software every day I know they make great image-editing software. I have also witnessed the company's smooth migration from CD-Rom and DVDs to a "cloud-based" subscription model. Adobe's cloud-based app updates save time and ensure that customers are always "up to date." Adobe bills monthly or yearly for use of their software, which is a terrific way for the company to ensure consistent revenues.

Based on my own experience as a loyal customer for about 20 years I have insights into the quality of the company's products and services and a belief (which could be wrong) that the company will likely produce the dominant image-editing software company for many years into the future.

Think about what you know because of your school, where you work, the people you know, or where you live. Which companies are doing well? Which companies do you admire and believe will grow in the future?

Where you live provides an edge

In addition to being a photographer, because I live in Seattle, I've witnessed the growth of Amazon and Starbucks before my very eyes. If I could build a time machine I'd go back 10 or 20 years and buy stock in either or both companies.

Starbucks stores always have high traffic and they serve as a central meeting spot for friends and people doing business. Their stores and offerings (food as well as coffee) have increased over the years.

With Amazon, it was not so obvious 10 or 20 years ago that the company would be the success that it is today[3], but as even the casual observer can see, they have come to dominate online retail and cloud computing.

I have seen Amazon and Starbucks grow before my eyes, and they would both have been excellent long-term investments. I'm not currently a shareholder in either company,[4] but these are the kind of long-term growing companies that make sense if you can see a company achieving massive success before your eyes. If you live close to some businesses that you see making great products or offering exceptional services (or both), then take a closer look at them. If you understand the businesses well and describe to another person why you believe the companies will succeed in the future, they may offer excellent investment opportunities.

In his book "One Up on Wall Street,[5]" Peter Lynch suggests investors buy the stock of companies that they understand based on their first-hand experience. His book is among the best I've read about investing, and I recommend adding it to your library when you're finished reading this.

A simple exercise you can do now

I'd like you to do an exercise right now because it will help you find your edge. Get a pen and a piece of paper (or use your phone or computer if you prefer) and write down your own edge. For example, if you love Nike sneakers and apparel, then you may have some degree of expertise when it comes to understanding demand for Nike products and how much customers admire their current styles, etc. If you have that strong feeling that the company has something powerful behind it then write "Nike" on your list and a few sentences about why.

If you worked at Victoria's Secret then you might have known that the chain of stores was struggling starting in 2017 and the problems continued to grow. You see, because you see store traffic and you know what customers are asking for (and whether they're buying it or going to American Eagle instead. There are many alternatives to Victoria's secret and you might know if customers are deserting stores and instead going to other brick and mortar stores or shopping on Amazon instead. So, if you work at Victoria's secret (or have friends who do) that is your edge. Write "Victoria's Secret" (or L Brands, who is the parent company that owns the brand) and a few sentences about the company.

I'll tell you right now about a company I don't own any stock in, but that I could easily put on my list of companies I understand. Apple Computer makes a lot of different devices, but the iPhone is king. When I get another phone it will be an iPhone, and most of my friends who have them will do the same.

In addition, Apple customers buy Air Pods, Apple Watches, iPads, MacBook Pros, etc. So there's this incredible "stickiness" to their products that ensures people will continue to buy them for the foreseeable future. If you use iPhones and love the products then you can put Apple on the list. If you don't then just write down some other company where you have an edge.

This will seem like a simple exercise, but it is powerful. You deciding on the few things where you can have deep knowledge will serve you well in life and investing.

In your daily life, you will hear about hot stocks from friends, online articles, newspapers, and stock newsletters that arrive in your inbox. You'll probably get excited about some of these stocks. Even if you think you are immune from crowd psychology just stay strong and before you tap and swipe and start buying stock, just ask yourself if it's on your list of companies where you have an edge. If you don't then you can't expect to get anything more than average returns on your investments. After all, why do you deserve to win big at investing if you don't know more than the next person?

Concentrate your energy on investigating companies where you possess an edge due to your unique experiences or effort you have spent to read, watch videos, or learn in any way you can about investments. This will help you deserve the success that will be yours through deep understanding.

15

BUFFETT ON HIS EDGE

"The most important thing is to be able to define which ones you can come to an intelligent decision on and which ones are beyond your capacity to evaluate. You don't have to be right about thousands and thousands and thousands of companies, you only have to be right about a couple."

— WARREN BUFFETT

Warren Buffett's best advice for investors is to stick to things they understand.

I recently watched a documentary titled, "Becoming Warren Buffett."[1] What stuck with me after watching that film is how selective Buffett is when it comes to buying stocks. He is careful not to overpay when buying stocks, and he says "no" when some company or situation is too hard for him to understand.

Buffett said there are all kinds of businesses that he doesn't understand, and the key to his success is not omniscience but selectivity. To illustrate this concept he referred to "The Science of

Hitting," a book by baseball great Ted William, with a diagram that shows Williams standing at home plate with a strike zone divided into 77 squares, each the size of a baseball.

Williams said that if he only swung at pitches in his sweet zone, outlined in the diagram, his batting average would be .400. "If he had to swing at low outside pitches — but still in the strike zone — his average would be .230," Buffett said. "He said the most important thing in hitting is waiting for the right pitch."

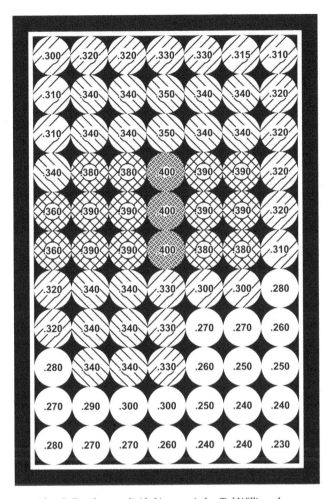

A baseball strike zone divided into 77 circles. Ted Williams knew he could hit with an impressive .400 batting average if he only swung at balls in his "sweet spot." All other circles represent lower batting averages from swinging at less desirable pitches. In baseball you must swing at any pitch in the "strike zone" or you can get called out on strikes. In investing, you can let pitch after pitch pass by, and you never get called out.

In baseball you have to swing at pitches in the strike zone — *even if you don't want to* — or you risk being called out on strikes. So, there is a penalty for waiting until you get the right pitch.

But you have an advantage with investing because *there are no called strikes.* You can just wait until you see the company you want to invest in selling for a price that makes sense to you.

Ted Williams was at a huge disadvantage because if the count was 0-2 or 1-2, even if that ball was down where he was going to bat .230 he still had to swing at it. Yet with investing, there are no called strikes, so people can throw Microsoft at you, Walmart, Bank of America, Starbucks, Target, Barrick Gold, Simon Property Group, Nike, Disney, Tesla, you name it, any stock, and *you don't have to swing.* Your advantage as an investor is that patience is rewarded, and you can't get called out on strikes.

"The trick in investing is just to sit there and watch pitch after pitch go by," Buffett said, "and wait for the one in your sweet spot, and when people are yelling 'swing you bum'...ignore 'em. There's a temptation for people to act far too frequently in stocks simply because they're so liquid," he said.

Buffett uses filters to help with stock selection. "Over the years you develop a lot of filters," he said. "And I do know what I call my circle of competence, so I stay within that circle. And I don't worry about things that are outside that circle. Defining what your game is — where you're going to have that edge — is enormously important.[2]"

This notion is something that Warren Buffett repeats and it doesn't get a lot of coverage in the press though it is profound. Since at least the 1990s, when visiting college students and giving advice on how to get rich, Buffett has often emphasized the importance of understanding a company before you invest.

"I could improve your ultimate financial welfare by giving you a ticket with only twenty slots in it so that you had twenty punches — representing all the investments that you got to make in a lifetime. And once you'd punched through the card, you couldn't make any more investments at all. Under those rules, you'd really think carefully about what you did, and you'd be forced to load up on what you'd really thought about. So you'd do so much better."

— WARREN BUFFETT

STOCK MARKET INTELLIGENCE

LIFETIME
STOCK
PUNCH CARD

○ 1._____	○ 11._____
○ 2._____	○ 12._____
○ 3._____	○ 13._____
○ 4._____	○ 14._____
○ 5._____	○ 15._____
○ 6._____	○ 16._____
○ 7._____	○ 17._____
○ 8._____	○ 18._____
○ 9._____	○ 19._____
○ 10._____	○ 20._____

*A punch card with 20 punches on it. Warren Buffett said that if
students got a punch card with 20 punches on it when they
graduated from school, and that is all the investment decisions
they got to make in their entire lives, they would get very rich
because they would think hard about each decision.*

"In fact," Buffett said, "I've told students if when they got out of school, they got a punch card with 20 punches on it, and that's all the investment decisions they got to make in their entire life, they would get very rich because they would think very hard about each one. And you don't need 20 right decisions to get very rich. You know, 4 or 5 will probably do it over time."

This punch card policy is simple and can change your investment results. Lou Simpson, whose job was to invest GEICO's stock portfolio, was one of the best investors in the world. Warren Buffett, who worked with Simpson for many years, said that his stocks often performed better than Buffett's selections.

Simpson says there is no mystery to his stock market magic. A voracious reader, he searches newspapers, magazines, annual reports and newsletters for clues that might spark investment ideas[3].

Speaking of Simpson, Warren Buffett said that his success is based on sticking to his principles.

"Lou has made me a lot of money," Buffett said. "Under today's circumstances, he is the best I know. He has done a lot better than I have done in the last few years. He has seen opportunities I have missed. We have $700 million of our own net worth of $2.4 billion invested in Geico's operations, and I have no say whatsoever in how Lou manages the investments. He sticks to his principles. Most people on Wall Street don't have principles to begin with. And if they have them, they don't stick to them.[4]"

Lou Simpson said he has five investment principles. They are listed below along with his quotes on each one:

1. *Think Independently.* "We try to be skeptical of conventional wisdom and try to avoid the waves of irrational behavior and emotion that periodically engulf Wall Street."

2. *Invest in High-Return Businesses Run for the Shareholders.* "Does management have a substantial stake in the stock of the company? Is management straightforward in dealings with the owners?"

3. *Pay only a reasonable price, even for an excellent business.* "We

try to be disciplined in the price we pay for ownership even in a demonstrably superior business."

4. *Invest for the long-term.* "Attempting to guess short-term swings in individual stocks, the stock market or the economy is not likely to produce consistently good results."

5. *Do not diversify excessively.* "An investor is not likely to obtain superior results by buying a broad cross-section of the market. The more diversification, the more performance is likely to be average, at best. We concentrate our holdings in a few companies that meet our investment criteria.

Simpson said that this particular "punch card" strategy helped him enormously in his record of crushing the market over several decades.

This strategy will appear in different chapters with different wording throughout the book, and that's because it works. While several of the explanations feature examples in text form, I like the punch card because its a strong visual representation of the maximum number of stocks you should consider in your lifetime.

Adhering to this rule will help you steer clear of messy situations and ensure that you to invest in your best ideas. This approach will also help you avoid excessive diversification, and will encourage you to spend more time learning about a company before investing.

16

WHAT DO YOU UNDERSTAND?

In an earlier chapter, you discovered where you have an edge based on your education, experience as a customer, your job, etc. Now that you have described your edge, it's time to identify specific companies.

Just to recap the exercise at the start of the book, you must make a list of companies that you understand well. You can choose as many as you'd like, but I think you'll be best off if you start with 10 or fewer companies. You can always add more to your list later.

Companies you understand

1.
2.
3.
4.
5.
6.
7.
8.
9.
10.

1. Now you have your list. It should be on a piece of paper, your laptop, or your phone. Just write it down.
2. Once you have written down the names of a few companies you are going to start learning more about them.
3. Go to the website of each company. Under the "Investor Relations" section find the most recent "annual report."

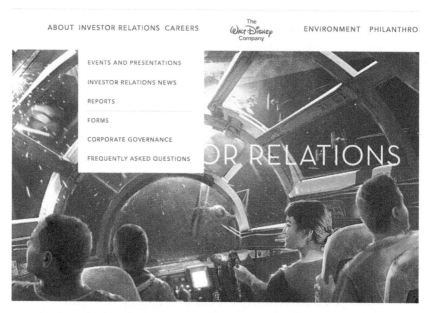

Screenshot from the Disney website. Click on the "INVESTOR RELATIONS" navigation button.

4. Download an annual report for each company on your list. It takes less than a minute per report. You can download the report easily by clicking the link, such as those pictured below on the Walt Disney Company's website.

Screenshot from the Walt Disney Company's investor relations page found on the company's website.

5. Read the annual report for the current year. It's the single most important document you can read to get a solid understanding of the company. I recommend reading several annual reports from the same company to get an idea of what the company has been doing in recent years, and their success in completing what they set out to do. The "Letter to Shareholders," written by the CEO, is packed with useful information about past accomplishments and plans for the future.

Once you've read the annual report you are ready to proceed. Even if you have not yet read the annual report, it's ok to read on...but really, before you invest in a company you owe it to yourself to read the annual report. You might even find it to be fun, and you'll surely learn a lot of cool things about the business.

Errors of commission and omission

The two mistakes you're most likely to make are either:

1. *Errors of commission* in which you do something by mistake that doesn't work out. This includes buying a stock when you don't understand the company well or when you buy stock and the economy changes dramatically and the company's prospects deteriorate. For example, buying airline, cruise, or hotel stocks right before the Coronavirus pandemic.

2. *Errors of omission* in which you don't act when you should. This includes understanding a company but waiting or never buying the stock because it seemed too expensive at the time, etc. This happens when you learn a lot about a company through reading, watching videos, or through your work and you suck your thumb instead of backing up the truck and loading up on the stock.

Most people who have invested for a while know the feeling of doing something stupid, and these are easy to forgive yourself for because everyone who invests for any length of time will make some mistakes.

The errors of omission can get you because you were prepared but did not act. When you know enough to make a solid decision but you just sit around and wait for a better price, which never arrives.

So, the cure to avoiding errors of omission is to wait until you feel confident in your understanding of a company, and then make a decision when you feel ready. You might not want to wait until you know 100% percent about a situation because that will never happen. Once you have about 70% of the information you need and it might be time to think about buying the stock.

My big error of omission

My mistake — if I'm honest in appraising my investing record over the past 10-15 years — is that I did not buy any stock in three companies I patronize most: Adobe, Amazon, and Apple. As a professional photographer, I've used Photoshop almost every day since 2003. Adobe is the best image-editing software around, yet I've never bought Adobe Systems stock. Big mistake.

I've owned only iPhones and MacBook Pro computers since I started buying Apple products in 2008 and I've never looked back. Every phone or computer I've bought since is made by Apple, and the same could be said of many of my friends. Yet I've never bought Apple Stock.

Finally, I've been an Amazon Prime member and a regular customer of Amazon's since around 2006 but never bought Amazon stock. This is probably the biggest non-decision I've ever made. I've seen the many benefits of buying things from Amazon over the years, and I've been a loyal customer. I've bought almost all of my cameras, lenses, and business equipment from Amazon over the last 15 years, yet I never bought Amazon stock.

Learn from my mistake: If you focus your research on companies that you understand well — especially through your direct experience as a customer — you will have an advantage. Also, look around you, and you may notice that a lot of other people are patronizing the same businesses and are very happy with the products and services.

Once you have created a list of companies you know well, then you'll be well-prepared to dive deep and ask the questions I'll teach you in upcoming chapters.

17

FOCUS IS KEY

G reat investors focus well. I am a photographer and investor, and both pursuits require patience, focus, and decisiveness. The same qualities are crucial to investing success. Learning about companies and waiting for the right stock price takes patience. As you become a more experienced investor you'll learn to focus by reading, learning, and following the progress of a company over time. It's not a boring or tedious process; it's exciting.

When Bill Gates first met Warren Buffett, their host at dinner, Gates's mother, asked everyone around the table to identify what they believed was the single most important factor in their success through life. Gates and Buffett gave the same one-word answer: "Focus."[1]

You will find it easy to focus once you start researching companies that you're fanatical about. Notice I didn't say "companies that interest you" or "companies that you like." You have to be a fanatic. You have to like learning, digging, and asking questions. In my experience, the best investors resemble investigative reporters — always asking questions to learn more.

By becoming a fanatic and focusing you narrow down your scope of view. You can't be an expert in everything, but you can become an expert in a few things and focus on them. You need to be able to devote attention to learning, avoid distractions, and become an expert on any company before you ever invest.

As we mentioned earlier, Todd Combs, who Warren Buffett hired to work at Berkshire as an investment manager, reads for 12 hours a day. That is what it takes to get an investment record so good that Buffett notices you. I'm not saying that you have to spend every waking hour learning about companies, but just notice the connection between time spent reading and learning and success.

Your ability to focus on what you understand, eliminate everything else, and get some serious reading and learning done will help you greatly. You have to become an expert and dive really deep. When you understand a company better than most other people, that will be a sign that you're getting somewhere. Once you become an expert in that company you need to be prepared to act decisively when prices get cheap.

One great way to ensure you're prepared is to always have a cash reserve in the bank ready to invest. As Charlie Munger explains, it can make all the difference. "Being prepared on a few occasions in a lifetime, to act promptly in scale, in doing some simple and logical thing, will often dramatically improve the financial results of that lifetime," he said.[2]

Focus on learning

Buffett was once asked the question, "What is your best advice for new investors?"[3]

"For a new investor, well I would do a lot of reading before I invested, I would prepare for it. I wouldn't just jump in the water 'till I thought I knew I could swim. So I did a lot of reading — I read every book that the Omaha public library had about investing by the time I was 11. You've got plenty of time, you're young, to invest, so why not go in prepared instead of learning as you go along. You

*will learn as you go along — that comes with investing, but it's
better if you've done some thinking about it, sort of take your time
getting into it. But you're not too young to start preparing for it at
all."*

— WARREN BUFFETT

Buffett's approach always leans toward learning, preparation, and understanding. These practices are greatly helped along by doing plenty of reading and watching lectures and interviews on YouTube and other video platforms. You would be amazed by the quality and quantity of videos by great investors, and also by the leaders of many of the companies you might be considering for investment.

The time you spend reading, learning, and viewing videos is part of the focus required to excel as an investor.

18

A GOOD CHECKLIST

"No wise pilot, no matter how great his talent and experience, fails to use his checklist."

— CHARLIE MUNGER

Once you start using the PALMS filtering system — essentially an investing checklist — you'll develop ninja-like speed and quickness when it comes to picking promising companies and weeding out the others. You won't even need to look at a printout. Just look at the palm of your hand.

As I mentioned earlier, before you even start the PALMS approach, make sure you understand the company you're considering.

This book teaches you a checklist and it's up to you to go through a company and answer each item yourself.

In his book "The Checklist Manifesto,"[1] Atul Gawande wrote:

"*Good checklists:*

... are precise. They are efficient, to the point, and easy to use even in the most difficult situations.

They do not try to spell out everything - a checklist cannot fly a plane.

They provide reminders of only the most critical and important steps - the ones that even the highly skilled professionals using them could miss.

Good checklists are, above all, practical."

Pilots use checklists because they virtually eliminate mistakes and oversights. Photo © Jeff Luke.

Professionals use checklists whenever lives are at stake, whether in the operating room or an airplane. "Pilots use checklists because they virtually eliminate mistakes and oversights. In addition to mechanical checklists mounted in the cockpit, we consult plasticized and electronic checklists displayed on computer screens, and checklists for tasks like de-icing.[2]"

Similarly, the PALMS filtering system provides a simple system to help you eliminate mistakes and decide if a stock makes sense. It's practical and easy to use, and you can always find the checklist by glancing at the palm of your hand.

You can use PALMS to make sure you aren't overlooking any important investment factors. However, I want to be clear with you that this is not a stock-picking formula because one doesn't exist. You must take your time and do your research; just think that because it requires hard work it's going to be a chore. I'm always learning new things when I learn about companies—new technologies, inventions, people, etc, and this process always makes me want to learn more.

I believe a framework is better than a general formula, which will not work for everyone. Why would the person who developed the formula share it with other people if they could keep the secret to themselves? There are books about investing that provide "magic formulas," but can we reasonably expect that every person who buys the book will find success? If everyone could use the formula it would get used so often that the advantage would disappear.

No, I think an investing framework makes sense. It shows you the investing factors and lets you find your way. It is not a roadmap to investment that will show you some straight path to success because no such map exists. You will discover stocks that make sense based on your understanding of the world.

The PALMS checklist is designed to keep you on track and asking the right questions. It should also prevent you from making mistakes.

Just say 'No'

Just say *no* to a lot of lousy investment ideas. If the company has never turned a profit, just say *no*. If you got a hot tip from someone and you know nothing about the company, just say no. Why on earth do you deserve to get rich investing in things that you know nothing about? Saying "no" keeps things simple and ensures that when you say *yes* you will mean it.

The more you use PALMS the more it will become instinctive, and it will always be there for you.

19

A RELIABLE SYSTEM

You need a reliable investing system comprised of a few simple factors. Those that pass are candidates and those that fail you can easily eliminate.

The next chapter will introduce you to a system that comes in the form of a simple checklist of five important factors you can run through to make sure a stock you're thinking of investing in meets certain criteria. You can think of this checklist as a kind of filter. Most stocks won't make it through the filter because it's so selective, yet those that pass through are decent candidates for investing. You will get better the more you read, prepare, and learn.

You want to invest in a rational, businesslike way and adopt a mindset where you stay calm and don't get too excited when the market goes up, nor too upset when it goes down. Your approach should be that of a cool captain, not swayed by emotions at some critical time. You will be such a wise, powerful investor once you adopt this system and get the hang of using it every time you consider a new investment.

Investing in stocks is like learning a new language. It takes time, and at first, everything seems new and exciting. Sometimes you might feel uncertain about what you're doing. Don't give up, and don't get frustrated. Just aim to go to bed a bit wiser than when you woke up. Read a lot, enjoy the process, ask for help if you need it, and you will get more fluent in the language of investing.

People ask me about stocks all the time. They say, "What do you think about Nvidia?" or "Do you think Tesla is a good investment?" They want me to give them tips to help them decide on which stocks to buy, but they don't know how to figure these things out themselves. They ask for advice the same way they would ask for a restaurant recommendation. I never tell people what stocks are best. It is much better to show people how to use the tools themselves so they can enjoy the process of learning. The best investors need to ignore the advice of other people who are often clueless. If you listen to others you will surely get confused, as most investors get swept up by emotion.

I'm writing this book to teach you a good system in which you ask a series of five questions about a company. You will learn to answer these questions yourself so you can make intelligent decisions about stocks. One interesting fact I will share is that the world's best investors, people like Warren Buffett and Charlie Munger, use filters all the time. It helps them quickly decide what stocks deserve more attention and which are belong in the pile marked "too hard" to understand.

My expertise comes from direct experience investing for more than 20 years, making a lot of mistakes, and learning from them. I designed a "filtering" system that you can use to decide if a stock makes sense for you. This system is based on five important questions, and when you answer them you will be able to decide if a stock makes sense as an investment.

I developed this filtering system out of necessity because I wanted a set of tools I could use to make high-quality decisions quickly. I am good at explaining complex things in simple ways, and I've applied this skill to explaining stock investing in a way that anyone can understand.

Five obstacles make investing difficult for beginners:

1. Most beginning investors have only seen the market go up. They believe that investing is easy, and all you have to do is put money into stocks and you will get rich. It is not easy to do something simple that takes little intelligence and become rich quickly. It's not easy to get rich quickly with stocks and stay rich. That is the mirage of a bull market when stocks seem to only go up.

2. When people are starting to invest they tend to rely on other people for stock tips and advice. Even though it's tempting to ask for advice, instead they will be better served by reading a lot and learning about companies themselves and then forming their own opinions. Good investing requires independent thought.

3. Beginning investors are not aware of the value of reading annual reports before they invest. All companies provide annual reports for free, and anyone can request a free copy mailed to them or can download them instantly from the "Investor Relations" section of the website. Most young investors I know buy stock without ever reading the annual report, which I believe is a serious mistake. The best investors read about companies constantly and they almost always start with the annual report.

4. Buying stocks is easier than ever before, but doing something quickly does not translate to doing it well. New apps make it easy to buy and sell stocks using your mobile phone, and why buying stocks is cheaper and faster than at any time in history, the ease of quick execution can make a beginning investor bypass the reading and learning necessary to make intelligent stock decisions.

5. The stock market has been hitting highs every year for almost 10 years. This is great for investment returns, but I believe beginning investors are going to (falsely) believe the stocks only go up. When the stock market eventually declines or crashes (and it always does) these new investors might be caught by surprise, unaware that things

can quickly take a turn for the worst. Many investors —
not just beginners, this happens all the time to
experienced investors — lose enormous amounts of
money in secret, anguishing experiences that they never
talk or write about because they were doing things they
never should have done.

This book will show you how to think for yourself, keep calm
under pressure, and use a simple checklist to filter out the stocks to
avoid so you can focus on those you understand.

I'd like to add that on the positive side, many beginning investors
today have discovered how to buy stocks online or by using mobile
phone apps like Robinhood to buy stock. I see this as a positive thing
because by buying just a few shares, new investors are learning
through the experience of "dipping their toes" in the investment
waters. Learning by doing is a good approach, as long as you only
invest small amounts so your bad decisions won't cost too much.

The first thing I want to share is that it's not likely that you will get
rich quickly in the stock market. It can take several years for your
stocks to do well. The hot stocks will not always go up. It's important
to have the proper mental framework to invest, and that means you
should be patient and not be discouraged by the stock market's short
term action.

Someone recently asked me, "What website do you use to get
investing information?" I don't rely on one financial website or even a
few of them. I try to get news from a variety of different sources
including *The Wall Street Journal*, *The New York Times*, and the *Financial Times*. I watch YouTube videos to learn more about companies,
and I like to watch interviews with CEOs to gauge their talent and
integrity.

I don't think it makes much sense to rely on any website or
market commentator for advice or guidance on what might happen
with the market. I don't think most talking heads know as much as
they suggest they might, and if they did I don't think they'd freely
share their valuable information with their viewers.

"If the reason people invest is to make money, then in seeking advice they are asking others to tell them how to make money. That idea has some element of naïveté."

— BENJAMIN GRAHAM, *"THE INTELLIGENT INVESTOR"*

It makes sense to start reading the annual reports of any companies that interest you. I explain how to download an annual report from a company's website earlier in this book[1]. You can also read newspapers, books, magazines, and read articles online about the companies who make and sell you the things you buy. The more you read and learn about a company the better informed you will become.

It is fine to keep current by reading the financial press and visit financial websites, but don't rely on them as the sole source of financial information. But if you're reading the same articles as other people then your results will be the same as theirs — average. If you want to become more intelligent than the crowd, then you will need to expose yourself to different sources of information.

Even great investors make mistakes

Warren Buffett bought a large amount of IBM stock for Berkshire Hathaway's portfolio in 2011. He had read about the company for many years but never bought it. Eventually, he invested in that company, writing in the annual report "It's not what you look at that matters, it's what you see," and years later he admitted that IBM was a bad investment and he explained, "I was wrong...IBM is a big strong company...but they've got big strong competitors too."[2]

I would guess that Buffett viewed IBM as a company that has been successful for the past 10, 20, 30, 40, and 50 years and he envisioned future dominance. What was not clear when he invested in IBM is that the company would have many competitors: Microsoft,

Google, Apple, and others. Those companies may have brighter futures than IBM because they are innovating and inventing new products and services for their customers faster than IBM.

I believe you can do much better than other investors if you adopt an approach that blends the sound thinking and a practical checklist with envisioning where innovative companies are going.

Don't follow the clueless crowd

Just because everyone else is clueless doesn't mean you have to be. Let other people buy Xerox and IBM. Let other people pay crazy high prices for tech stocks that have shot up far too high simply because their friend told them about it. You don't need to buy companies with rich histories but hazy futures. You don't need to buy overpriced, overhyped companies.

What you need is a process — a simple checklist that you can run through that will help you to figure out quickly if a stock makes sense — not for your best friend, neighbor, the guy touting stocks on t.v. or the financial journalist in the online finance site or your favorite money podcast.

The stocks you think of buying will make much more sense when you understand the underlying companies and can picture how and why they will grow in the future.

Every stock is a story

You may remember that at the start of this book I quoted Peter Lynch, who said: "If you're prepared to invest in a company, then you ought to be able to explain why in simple language that a fifth-grader could understand, and quickly enough so the fifth grader won't get bored."[3]

As you read the rest of this book, you will be asking yourself five questions about each company you consider for investment. I want to encourage you to start thinking about any company as a kind of "investigative reporter" who is trying to uncover information. Eventually, you will want to understand the "story" well enough that you can explain it simply and clearly to others.

The better you are at explaining your stocks to others in a simple way, the more you'll know you understand them yourself. Investing is not that complex or confusing. You will find that asking questions, being patient while you find the answers, and learning to tell a story a company is a great way to make sure you understand what you're doing every step of the way.

PART IV

INVESTING WISDOM: GET INSPIRED BY
THE GREATS

20

THE MAGIC BOX

"Einstein is credited with saying compound interest is the most powerful force in the universe. The notion of putting money away is most important to the cohort that least understands it: young people."

— SCOTT GALLOWAY

The magic box

Compound interest is the key to investing. Charlie Munger said, "Understanding both the power of compound interest and the difficulty of getting it is the heart and soul of understanding a lot of things."

"Start putting away money, early and often. Think of it as magic. Put $1,000 into a magic box and in 40 years — BOOM! — it's $10,000 to $25,000. If you could have this magic box, how much money would you put in it?[1]"

If you had this magic box and put $1,000 into it so that in 40 years it's $10,000 to $25,000, how much money would you put in it? Photo © Jeff Luke

The idea of a magic box into which you put money is that the value of your shareholder equity — your ownership of the business through stocks — will increase if the company can successfully compound shareholder equity at an attractive rate over the long term. The growth of your part of shareholder equity (reflected in the price of your stock) over time is called compound interest.

You should seek to invest in companies with great prospects to grow over the years because your investment returns will not be much different than the returns on the companies returns on capital. If they just buy tools or equipment with their profits, the business won't grow. You want to invest in companies that generate lots of extra cash and invest it intelligently.

"Over the long term, it's hard for a stock to earn a much better return than the business which underlies it earns," Charlie Munger said.[2] "If the business earns 6% on capital over 40 years and you hold it for that 40 years, you're not going to make much different than a 6%

return—even if you originally buy it at a huge discount. Conversely, if a business earns 18% on capital over 20 or 30 years, even if you pay an expensive looking price, you'll end up with a fine result," he said.

Compound Interest

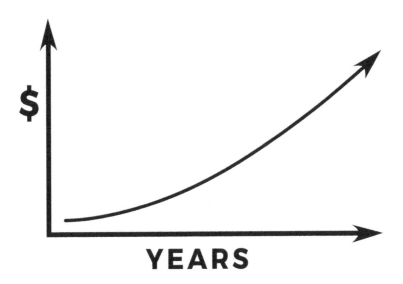

Einstein is credited with saying that compound interest is the most powerful force in the universe, and Ben Franklin wrote, "Remember that money is of a prolific generating nature. Money can beget money, and its offspring can beget more, and so on."

Some people are more patient than others and are born with a temperament that's well-suited for investment. Patience followed by decisiveness on a few occasions in life is a good recipe for success. Even if you are not naturally a patient person, or you lack decisiveness you can develop these qualities over time to become a better investor.

It's safe to say, however, that not all people are patient investors; the human brain is not wired to be patient. Humans evolved because our large brains gave us the ability to make quick decisions based on fight or flight. We react to threats in our surroundings as a matter of survival, but there is little reward in nature for patience. The instinct to *do things* is hard-wired into us. *We are not built to sit around and do nothing.*

Yet, emotion-based thinking is our worst enemy when it comes to investing. We need to make fewer decisions because inaction is what lets your investments compound over time.

During the 2020 pandemic I have followed the investing channel of a YouTuber in his 30s. He had all of his money in stocks, and these investments had done well over time. He remained calm during the stock market crash in March, and to his credit he remained patient and did not sell his stocks, but he made a serous mistake soon after the recovery began: he sold all of his stocks in May of 2020 and went to cash because he thought too much about the pandemic and decided the market had recovered too quickly and would likely crash again.

He sold his stocks and went to cash after the market had recovered about 10%, but the market continued to climb 30% more in the next two months. If he had done nothing his investments would have grown 30% more in two months.

The other problem he has is that now the markets have recovered to near all-time highs, and stocks are now more expensive than ever. If he wants to get back into the market he will have to buy back in when stocks are much more expensive.

His emotional decision to sell stocks caused him to "sell low" and if he ever wants to invest again he may have to "buy high." His decision to time the market presents a paradox: he can pay inflated prices to reinvest now that stocks are more expensive, or sit on the sidelines as the market climbs in the future. It's a no-win situation. One event in his favor would be a stock market crash, but what kind of life is it to just walk around hoping the market crashes.

Charlie Munger presented the model he called "Sit on your ass investing" at the 2000 Berkshire Hathaway annual meeting. Munger said, "All you have to do is pick a really great company when it is attractively priced, and then just sit on your ass. The great advantage being that it only requires one decision."

To invest intelligently, your goal should be to let compound interest occur and never interrupt it unnecessarily. There are are many ways to interrupt it, such as selling stock or fund shares or switching (unnecessarily) from one investment to another. You can also buy a stock, for example, that loses a lot of its value.

In 2018 Facebook stock traded above $215 early in the year and then dropped below $125 later the same year. Similarly, Nvidia traded above $290 only to fall below $125 later in the year. People buying these stocks were likely just hoping the prices would keep going up, which is gambling. If they had been patient and not reacted to the stock prices going higher and higher they could have waited and bought the same shares much cheaper after the prices declined.

Overpaying for stocks is a sure way to destroy the effects of compound interest. If you pay a high enough price for a stock, it may never recover to the price you paid, or it could take so long just to break even that all of the years you wait are wasted because the money is not compounding over time.

The key takeaway from this chapter is to make a few good investments — it could be one, two, three stocks if you are just getting started. Learn as much as you can, buy your stocks, and don't feel you need to take action for the sake of doing something. Just aim to buy a few good stocks and let your money compound in value over time.

Munger put it best: "The whole idea of not having to do something extraordinary is one all investors should heed, yet it is easy to forget, particularly in stressful situations." Munger often says that investors do not have to do anything remarkable.

One of the most valuable lessons Munger offers to us to reduce your risk of downside loss. "It is remarkable how much long-term advantage people like us have gotten by trying to be consistently not stupid, instead of trying to be very intelligent," he said.

21

EYE ON ETERNITY

"You must look at things in the aspect of eternity.

— BARUCH SPINOZA

Think about owning shares of a company for a long time — 5, 10, 20 years or more. With this time frame, even if you don't get the absolute lowest price when you buy a stock, the company will grow with time and your investment will work out sell even if the purchase price was slightly expensive. In other words, it makes sense to pay a little more for the stock of a quality company.

Stock prices tend to follow company profits. At first glance, you might not want to buy the stock if the price seems high. It is hard to be disciplined and patient when you want to buy a stock, but the price seems too high. I was talking with a friend recently, and she told me that she remembers thinking of buying Amazon stock when it cost $200 a share. She didn't buy it then, but she did buy it years later when it cost $800 a share. She said that at $200 Amazon was a book store that did some other things, but at $800 it was obvious that Amazon was executing successfully in many different industries.

One of the keys to intelligent investing is the ability to spot companies like Amazon at $200 and being able to grasp the company's solid leadership and vision for the future. Many companies have big dreams for future success but are not able to execute on them. Once you find a company like that, keep in mind that there will be some very rough patches of poor stock performance and times when the market crashes and the stock declines in value. During these times, if the company is still intact and well-run, you need to keep a long-term view and resist selling merely because the price becomes cheap; this is precisely the time you might want to buy more stock.

If you go back and look at Amazon's 1997 Annual Report you can see a blueprint for what they would soon achieve. Even though many casual observers saw an online bookstore, Jeff Bezos spelled out his plans to those who read this letter.

"To our shareholders:

Amazon.com passed many milestones in 1997: by year-end, we had served more than 1.5 million customers, yielding 838% revenue growth to $147.8 million, and extended our market leadership despite aggressive competitive entry. But this is Day 1 for the Internet and, if we execute well, for Amazon.com. Today, online commerce saves customers money and precious time. Tomorrow, through personalization, online commerce will accelerate the very process of discovery. Amazon.com uses the Internet to create real value for its customers and, by doing so, hopes to create an enduring franchise, even in established and large markets..."

— *1997 Amazon Shareholder Letter by Jeff Bezos*

We can see that Amazon carried out its long-term vision successfully for more than 20 years. An investor who recognized the signs of success early on and bought stock would get great returns. You don't need to own many stocks like Amazon to make an excellent investing career.

One quality that sets Amazon apart from other companies is that it has never been overly concerned with appeasing short-term shareholder demands. Many companies try to impress investors by maximizing quarterly results at all costs or paying out a consistent dividend. They are focused on short-term performance that often gooses the CEO and executive team's bonuses.

Bezos and his team have focused first on their customers, and then on Amazon's culture of innovation and creating value for the long term. As a result, the company has attracted the kinds of shareholders who stuck around in years before the company had such tremendous success because they could see the architect's blueprint coming to life before their eyes.

Two of Amazon's leadership principles are to think long term and invent on behalf of customers, and the company emphasizes those principles even if that means they don't show a profit right away. When faced with showing a profit or reinvesting money in the business they choose the latter. It takes discipline to reinvest in the company when so many investors are focused on short-term profits. Therefore, thinking long term not only serves Amazon well, but it's also a good motto for the company's shareholders too.

However, intelligent investors can see progress before it's widely apparent to everyone else. For example, I've been a customer of Amazon's, buying many products other than books — cameras, lenses, furniture, etc., and while it's true I never invested in the company when it was not yet turning a profit, it hit a point a few years back when it became profitable. That was still an excellent time to invest in Amazon. The company was growing and profiting at the same time, and the early years of investment without profits were a thing of the past.

Bezos knows that thinking long term is essential. In the 1997 Amazon Shareholder Letter, he wrote, "*We believe that a fundamental measure of our success will be the shareholder value we create over the long term. This value will be a direct result of our ability to extend and solidify our current market leadership position. The stronger our market leadership, the more powerful our economic model."*

It's all laid out right in that one letter: Amazon had the vision to become the market leader early on. It was written in 1997 and the company has built upon it every year since.

So, how should knowing about this affect you as an investor? Well, you want to look for this kind of vision in any potential founder or CEO of a company in which you invest. I can't say that you will find someone just like Jeff Bezos, but you can find similar long-term focus and customer obsession.

For example, I did a lot of research into small companies for a book I wrote in 2019, the year before the Coronavirus pandemic. I discovered this small public company called Zoom Video Communications (ZM) and read a lot about its founder and CEO, Eric Yuan.

I watched several interviews with him on YouTube — there all still there — and the more videos I watched the more impressed I became with his talent and integrity. He focused on making his customers happy and making Zoom a great place to work.

While Eric Yuan and Jeff Bezos lead different companies, there is something hard to quantify but very powerful in their presence. Once you see that unique focus on customers and vision for the future it just jumps out at you.

The same long-term thinking that drives business benefits an investor as well. An investor needs to look past short-term noise and look further down the road, as far as possible when imagining how a business might look beyond the next 3, 5, or 10 years. Ben Graham encouraged his students to think long term at the start of his investing class at Columbia.

"Ben Graham opened the course by saying, 'If you want to make money on Wall Street you must have the proper psychological attitude. No one expresses it better than Spinoza the philosopher. Spinoza said, 'You must look at things in the aspect of eternity.'"[1]

— MARSHALL WEINBERG

Let's say you want to invest for the long term and you're not very sure if you should buy the stock. For one reason or another, you might hesitate and put off investing. It's natural to want to avoid making a mistake and sometimes this will prevent you from making that initial investment.

One way to get momentum to invest in a new company is to buy a small number of shares to start. You don't have to go "all in" at the beginning. You can just buy one share, or 10 shares or however many shares makes sense to you.

Once you've established a small position you can assess the company's progress and decide if you want to buy more shares. This way you can at least get started investing with an eye toward eternity. As time passes you'll figure out if you made a good decision, and if all goes well you can buy more shares later.

22

IDEAS FROM GREAT INVESTORS

"*Through chances various, through all vicissitudes, we make our way*"

— *AENEID*

S ome concepts can help readers harness a useful investing mindset. Investing is easy, but it helps if you know why you're doing it. Usually the answer "to make money" doesn't go far enough. If that was all you wanted you might get distracted and lose interest.

You need a driving force, a reason to invest. An interviewer once asked Warren Buffett, "What appealed to you about being rich?"[1] "Well, I like to be independent," Buffett said. "I want to be able to do what I want to do every day. And money lets you do that."

An interviewer asked Carol Loomis to describe Buffett's biggest strength.[2] "*Well, his biggest strength, without a doubt, is his rationality that he brings to business and investing,*" Loomis said. "*And this is a trait — rationality — that you would think many investors would bring to their work, but the fact is, most of them are swept up by emotions most of the time at some crucial time — and he never does that."*

The other psychological concept that helped me invest during the stock market collapse that happened during the Coronavirus Pandemic was to not fear the short term. I lifted my eyes from what was happening on the ground in front of me, and I lifted my gaze to the horizon. I thought of something that Buffett said about investing.

"American business is going to be worth more over time. That's what you're buying is a business — you're not buying a stock, you're buying a piece of a whole bunch of businesses. Are those businesses going to be worth more 10 or 20 or 30 or 40 years from now? Of course they are."

— WARREN BUFFETT

The quote above captures the long-term vision necessary to be a successful investor. If you buy stock in great businesses, you don't have to worry about getting selling it. If you do your research and buy wisely, you can just sit back and hold your stocks forever as they increase in value.

This takes the pressure off of you because you don't have to worry about the news, about what the market's doing today or this week or this year. You just buy the company and forget about the market.

Now I'm not suggesting you stick your head in the sand like an ostrich. Of course, you will pay attention to the news and your portfolio, but *you don't have to do anything.*

These stocks will compound in value for 10, 20, 30 years and beyond. You are not only investing for yourself but if you do things right you're investing for your children and future generations.

It will help you maintain the long-term view if you can have the right temperament. As Buffett said at the 2020 Berkshire Hathaway

Annual Meeting, "Fear is the most contagious disease you can imagine.[3]" So one of your main tasks as an investor is to insulate you from fear and other emotions that will sabotage your efforts. You want to keep cool and only react to the extent that you can take advantage of stock market collapses to buy stocks when they get cheap.

23

WE'RE ALL INDEXERS

"We're All Indexers"

— *JACK BOGLE*

Picking stocks using the filtering system in this book is not for everyone. Some people don't want to spend the time learning about companies who would be better off investing with low-cost index funds.

Many beginning investors would be better off buying a low-cost index fund rather than trying to pick stocks themselves. What I'm writing about in this book is directed toward people who want to bring more intensity to the game. I am not trying to fool you into thinking it's easy to beat the market and you can do it if you try.

I hope by now readers will understand that beating the market is extremely difficult. It takes skill, luck, the right temperament, and a willingness to continually learn about new companies. It also requires a mindset where you realize you're going to make some mistakes and lose money, but you will not be deterred by your mistakes; in fact, you'll look at each mistake as an opportunity to pick failure's pocket and learn something from each mistake.

Let's take a closer look at index investing. When you buy shares of an index fund you are buying a small part of many different companies. It's a simple way to own the entire universe of stocks — or any subset of the market — in one simple investment.

Now, keep in mind that if you an individual stock, somebody else is selling it; it's a closed universe. In that sense, we are all indexers because we're trading the same universe of stocks with one another.

Jack Bogle framed the foolishness of trying to outsmart other investors. "Look at the total stock market: that's what we all own," he said. "Now slice about a third of that out, and those are indexers who know the value of indexing, so they own an index fund, and with no trading," he said. "Then look at the other two thirds: those people own the market index, by definition, those stockholders, but they're not satisfied with that. They want to bet against each other, and therefore they lose to the index by the amount of transaction costs they have."

This chart shows the entire universe of stocks. Those are the stocks that all investors own. You can slice a third of that out and see that those investors know the value of indexing. Active investors and index investors are all fishing from the same stock universe.

One simple truth about investing is that we are all investing in the same companies. If you just look at the universe of companies in the United States, there are about 4,300 publicly traded companies.[1]

When you decide to buy a stock, at that same moment someone else decides to sell. It's hard to know at that moment if you've made the right decision, yet there are two expenses you'll have to pay for sure: trading commissions and taxes. These frictional costs eat away from your investment returns.

Invest with your eyes wide open. Realize that you are buying stocks in the same universe as everyone else. It's not easy to beat the average investor, especially when you consider the frictional costs of trading fees and taxes.

24

MY INVESTING MISTAKES

I've made my share of investing mistakes, and I felt horrible about them all. I have owned two stocks that sucked like an airplane toilet, and the sinking feeling of owning them lasted until the day I finally sold them. It's not a fun experience, but it's instructive.

I describe them in this chapter because you should know that even the author of an investing book makes mistakes. There are also a few key lessons that you can learn right now that could prevent you from making the same (or similar) mistakes. This is *real money* that you don't have to lose. That is huge news, and you can truly benefit by reading this book if you just sidestep a few breathtaking losses in the stock market.

The lessons that stick are often learned through trial and error. You tell yourself "I will never make this mistake again!" and learning this way will make things stick in your memory. It's better to make your mistakes when you're young and have less money to lose than when you're older and your losses are larger. Of course, it's better to learn from others' mistakes, but in the real world, it seems inevitable that you'll make your own mistakes. I hope that they are few, and the amounts of any losses are small.

All the books and articles you read about investing can only give you so much wisdom. Unfortunately, the lessons that stick can only be learned through direct experience. So if you can just learn not to panic, not to get flustered, and keep calm you'll be fine. Thinking of mistakes as a way to learn is a great approach. The important thing is to actually write down, or somehow make a note of what you learn from each mistake. If you forget them and repeat them, then you're going to be in trouble. But if you can pick the pocket of each mistake you make then you'll do well.

I wrote this chapter because I want to show you that even an experienced investor makes mistakes. This is not something that I feel good about sharing, but I feel that if I write a book about how to invest but don't discuss the mistakes I've made, you might (1) think I only make good decisions, which is not the case and (2) you will not realize how much you can learn from the market's feedback.

You will become an expert in identifying disastrous investments and avoiding them. Not shooting yourself in the foot as an investor is half the battle! So you want to avoid certain activities entirely and learn to deal with errors in judgment promptly when they arise.

The nuggets of truth in this chapter are that all successful investors if they've been at it long enough, have made mistakes. This chapter is merely shining a light on a few I've made to show you that you can make some dumb mistakes and still survive. You will learn from those mistakes (at least that should be your goal) and what you learn will make you an even better, stronger, and more intelligent investor.

You can also see some of the mistakes I made because I didn't have a system. I didn't realize the importance of any of the aspects of the PALMS system when I started, so everything I shared earlier in this book was not given to me at the start. Through not under-standing enough about businesses and not asking enough questions, I wound up making some painful mistakes. I've sorted things out and moved on with my investing (free to make even bigger and more horrible mistakes!) and I know you can benefit from learning about my bad decisions and not repeating them yourself.

The main risk I faced when starting was not knowing anything about investing! I was about 25 years old and just starting as a photographer in Seattle. I knew I wanted to invest but did not have many examples of successful investors. I had an optometrist who made a copy of a magazine article for me to read (it was very helpful getting started), but you have to realize that this was the mid-1990s and the Internet was brand new. Google and YouTube didn't exist yet, and there was no way to learn about investing online.

The first mutual fund I invested in was run by an experienced value investor, Michael Price. I chose the fund because it invested in stocks that were selling cheaply relative to their value. It turned out to be a great first fund because I started out investing in the years leading up to the dot com bubble and tech stock crash in 2000. The mutual fund did not participate in the speculative behavior and as a result, it did quite well.

After a few years, I also started investing in the Dodge & Cox Stock fund, a conservatively managed stock fund, and that fund also avoided the speculative excesses of the time. You have to realize that most of the hot money was pouring into tech funds like those run by the Janus Fund family, and those shareholders suffered miserably during the crash.

So you may be asking, what's the big deal, where's the mistake? Well, I hadn't made any big mistakes yet. I decided to start investing in the Vanguard 500 index. I believe this was because it was commonly known as a low-cost mutual fund, and it seemed like a great way to get exposure to "growth" stocks (because my other mutual funds were both "value" funds. The decision to buy shares of this fund was excellent; my mistake was that I decided to eventually sell my shares in the S&P 500 fund (which invests in the 500 largest US companies) and use the proceeds to purchase just two stocks.

If I had simply held my shares of the index fund I would have compounded my investing dollars at a much faster rate. Yet I was confident in my decision and it seemed smart at the time. I was pretty confident both stocks would do at least as well as, and probably much better than the index fund. That turned out to be a misjudgment and a bad mistake.

Here's the thing: when you're investing correctly, it should be boring. When I decided to sell my index fund and buy stocks I was overconfident from my success picking mutual funds and thought this ability would translate to stock picking: it did not. One truth I learned the hard way was that in my early years I was better at picking mutual funds than investing in stocks.

Now, 15 years later, I feel I can accurately explain what happened.

1. My mutual funds were rolling along, compounding in value, and I got bored. I felt the need to buy some stocks and "hit it big" with a few wins.
2. My mutual funds were doing great, and I assumed my good fund decisions would translate to outstanding stock selections.
3. I thought I understood the stocks I was buying, but in reality, I knew little about the underlying companies or their leaders.

Let me give you a little background about a couple of horrible decisions that I made, and something I've learned from my mistakes. I'm hoping you can learn a valuable lesson from my experience so you don't repeat it yourself.

The year was 2004 and for the past few years, I'd been buying many shares of the Vanguard S&P 500 index fund. I had been investing $200 every month and it compounded in value. Instead of being happy with my index funds' success, which took very little effort on my part, I decided to improve on the perfectly decent 10.4% return of the Vanguard S&P 500 index fund that year. Instead of sticking with index funds, I figured I'd try my hand at picking stocks and beat the boring S&P 500 index fund.

So, at the end of the year, I sold all of my Vanguard index fund shares and used the proceeds to buy two stocks.[1] Yes, you read that correctly. I decided to put all of my eggs in *only two baskets*. I went from 500 companies in the index fund to owning just two stocks.

Here are the two stocks that I bought:

Stock 1: Leucadia National Corporation

I made a gamble on this company mainly because I understood next to nothing about what this company did. I thought you could be "close enough" in understanding a stock. I knew that historically the stock had performed well, and I had heard that the CEO, Ian Cumming, was a well-respected dealmaker.

Leucadia National Corporation had frequently been referred to as a "Baby Berkshire Hathaway" and it was run by two experienced investors, Cumming and Joseph Steinberg. In retrospect, the comparison to Berkshire Hathaway was a stretch because Berkshire Hathaway buys quality companies with strong competitive "moats," and Leucadia's managers bought cheap, disheveled, and out-of-favor companies, nursed them back to health, and sold them at a big profit. In real estate parlance, they were good at "flipping" companies.

Shortly after I bought the stock their success changed. They experienced several small failures, one success (an investment in an Australian mining company called Fortescue), and then the company went off the rails after the financial crisis. Leucadia has not participated in the stock market recovery since 2009. Leucadia National stock has underperformed the S&P 500 index eight of 10 years from 2010-2020, trailing the index by as much as -32.86% in 2014.[2]

Leucadia invested in a biotech start-up called Sangart that researched a synthetic blood substitute that could be used in trauma situations such as car accidents or in combat where patients need blood immediately and human blood is not available for transfusions. Sangart developed a substance called Hemospan that was also known as MP4OX). This substance was a Polyethylene glycol-conjugated human hemoglobin. This blood substitute participated in clinical trials in the US and Europe. In animal models, Hemospan was shown to be effective in cases of hemorrhagic shock[3].

There was a lot of hope that Hemospan would be a blockbuster red blood cell substitute as it was capable of transporting large amounts of oxygen. Sangart announced positive results from a phase II study for this product in November 2005.

Over many years, Leucadia invested hundreds of millions of dollars in Sangart, and eventually owned the entire company. If Hemospan had been a blockbuster the gamble would have paid off, but in the end, the blood substitute was not approved by the FDA and Sangart immediately shut down its business. The hemospan dream died and there was nothing to show for the investment.

Though it was only one of Leucadia's many investments, I feel Sangart epitomized Leucadia's downfall. In its early days the ball bounced in their favor, but when things start going bad the failures accelerate, and Sangart was the icing on the cake of bad investments.

Leucadia was not done yet. The company's last hurrah was the purchase of 78.95% of National Beef Packing Company for $867.9 million. Shortly after buying a majority interest in that business, the beef industry hit hard times. The cattle herd in the United States began to dwindle and the price of beef declined, which decreased revenues and profits in the beef processing industry.

Leucadia's CEO Ian Cumming and Chairman Joseph Steinberg decided it was time to retire from Leucadia, so they engineered a deal in which they merged Leucadia with an investment bank called Jefferies Group, which was run by CEO Richard Handler, who they admired and had worked with on many deals in the past. The combined company would retain the Leucadia name. In proposing the deal to shareholders, the leaders of both companies spoke of synergies in the deal where Jefferies (an investment bank) would provide Leucadia with special investment opportunities, and cash-rich Leucadia would provide Jefferies with the cash-rich fortress of a balance sheet that Jefferies desperately needed.

The synergies discussed before the merger never materialized. I held the stock for five years after the merger, all the while hoping the combined entity would meet up to the expectations set by the leaders who engineered the merger.

After owning Leucadia stock for more than a decade, I sold my shares at the same price — $23 a share — that I had bought them for a decade earlier. While I did not lose money in my Leucadia invest-ment, I would have fared better had I just left the money in the

Vanguard S&P 500 index fund, which returned 74% during the same time frame.

As a footnote to this debacle, though I sold my position in 2014, I noticed that Jefferies Group CEO Richard Handler (Leucadia National changed its name to Jefferies) was profiled in the Wall Street Journal as the highest paid banking and financial CEO in 2018 earning a total of $44,674,231.

He received this compensation despite his company lagging the S&P 500 by -13.19% over the past decade[4]. An article entitled, "Wall Street Chiefs' Pay Doesn't Sync With Returns" describes the discrepancy between the CEO pay and stock returns.[5]

Lessons learned: Just because you read that a company is like a "Baby Berkshire Hathaway" does not mean it's true. Even if seemingly smart mutual fund managers own the stock, that doesn't mean it's a good idea. I need to arrive at an understanding on my own, and not merely trust that the company's jockeys will continue to win their races, no matter how smart they seem. When a company faces one disappointment after another, it's a good idea to cut your losses and move on. There are better uses of time and money than hoping and waiting for brighter days.

Stock 2: White Mountains Insurance Group

White Mountains Insurance had an excellent history under its founder, Jack Byrne, who was a legend in the insurance world. I bought this stock mainly because I had heard how much Warren Buffett admired Jack Byrne (they had worked together in the past, during a time when Byrne saved GEICO from bankruptcy) and spoke incredibly highly of Byrne's abilities. So when I invested in White Mountains I thought I was becoming a shareholder in a conservatively run company with a great CEO.

Three years after I became an investor in White Mountains Jack Byrne stepped down as CEO and was replaced with a successor. I can't tell you much about what happened with the company after Byrne left, but like many insurance companies, White Mountains Insurance seemed like a boring business. That's to be expected because insurance companies are not as exciting as Wimbledon finals. Insurers collect premiums (called "float") and get to hold onto that money and invest it before they eventually have to pay claims, which may be years in the future. Insurance companies can break even on underwriting, but still make profits by investing the float. The *truly great insurers* make a profit on underwriting *and* by investing the float.

I don't really know if this particular insurance company was well-run because I didn't understand the calculations necessary to evaluate their business. It takes time to learn about the different segments of the insurance business (insurance, reinsurance, underwriting, investing) and I had not interest in becoming an expert on insurance.

Investing in an insurance company might make sense for an investor who already had experience in this industry. Over time I could see that the stock price of White Mountains Insurance Group was not keeping up with the S&P 500 index, and after a few years I decided to sell the stock because I didn't know if the bad relative performance was related to management, a bad climate for insurers, or something else.

Lessons learned: Because I didn't understand White Mountains Insurance or the insurance industry in general, I should not have invested in the company. When Jack Byrne, who did a fantastic job running the company decided to retire, I should have sold the stock. Continuing to hold the stock when the leader who built the great record departs can be a mistake.

What were my stock returns?

Though I was confident I could pick great stocks, I was not competent and I have proof from mediocre investment returns to prove it. Leucadia's 10-year average annual returns[6] were -5.66%. White Mountain Insurance Group's 10-year returns were 7.77%. The average annualized combined return for both companies during the previous 10-

year period was 1.06%. Now, I like a positive return as much as anyone, but that's not what I call a big move.

I didn't lose money, but I lost out on the opportunity to have that money invested in other businesses I understood.

I take responsibility for those returns. I chose the stocks when I bought them, and if things had turned out differently and their prices shot up to the moon I would have thought myself pretty smart. As it turned out the returns were mediocre at best, and I own those results. That's the only way I can learn from the situation. Of course, I could blame the lousy results on bad luck, but I wouldn't get to learn anything.

Even though I didn't lose money it was a pretty bad investment considering I took the risk of owning stocks and got worse returns than money in the bank. To show you the opportunity cost of my decisions, during the same 10-year period[7] the Vanguard S&P 500 index fund returned 10.37%.

The opportunity cost of my horrible decision was a decade's loss of compound interest. The money would have grown at a terrific rate if I'd just left it in the index fund. Instead, by selling my index fund shares (1) I had to pay capital gains taxes and (2) For more than a decade I had accepted stock-like risk in exchange for money market returns. The return of 1% did not keep pace with inflation, so my dollars lost purchasing power.

I interrupted the powerful effects of compound interest. It was like jamming a stick in my my spokes while riding a bike. I inflicted unnecessary harm when I could have done nothing.

My "take-home" lessons

The S&P 500 index fund is an excellent vehicle for compounding money over time, and my decision to sell my index fund shares to buy individual stocks was a bad idea at the time because I did not know enough about the companies I decided to buy. I needed to understand those two stocks on a much deeper level. I had not done enough research, and it was what I didn't know that seriously hurt my returns.

Warren Buffett says, "risk comes from not knowing what you're doing" and also "the best way to minimize risk is to think." I thought I had a good understanding of those two stocks but I did not. I knew about 5% of what I needed to know. I had a basic outline of the company after reading the annual report, but that wasn't enough.

In the future, I will invest only in stocks where I understand the business based on my research or direct experience as a customer. I will make sure any company is profitable, adaptable, has loyal customers, a moat, and is selling at a sensible price.

I think it's important to re-evaluate your reasons for buying a stock if the company's CEO changes, or if the company merges with another company. If the departing leader guided the company's past success, you may want to sell when they leave. If you wait too long you might wish you had sold sooner.

"Should you find yourself in a chronically leaking boat, energy devoted to changing vessels is likely to be more productive than energy devoted to patching leaks."

— WARREN BUFFETT

Pay no attention to any CEO statements about how they plan to turn things around in the future. Many leaders talk a good game, but promises of a brighter future are often based on optimism, not reality.

I'll give you an example of why I believe it's important to pay attention to the jockey running the company. Starbucks had a great run when its founder, Howard Schultz, led the company as CEO.

Schultz retired in 2000, and soon after he left , Starbucks lost its way. Same-store sales stagnated and the stock price went nowhere for three years. The perception of Starbucks as a high-end cafe waned and it seemed the brand had become boring; the qualities that made the cafes special had vanished. Things got so bad for Starbucks that Shultz came out of retirement and took over as CEO in 2008 after an eight-year hiatus. He remained at the company for eight years and helped get Starbucks back on track.

When Schultz stepped down again in 2016 he was replaced by Kevin Johnson, and the company seems to have recovered. Starbucks is an example of a company that is dependent on a leader for success. It is not enough for Starbucks to sell coffee. The brand is dependent upon a leader to build the culture and perception of the brand as a special destination. It's clear that Starbucks will not succeed under any leader — it needs someone who continues to provide a high-end customer experience and perception of gourmet coffee.

An intelligent investor must keep on top of leadership changes at any company they own or are considering for investment, and consider selling the stock — or at least monitor the situation carefully — when a new CEO takes the place of the company's founder.

Why did Starbucks fall on hard times? Part of the reason could be attributable to the founder's departure, but another explanation could be that the company grew rapidly for many years, and eventually that growth slowed. People eventually max out on how much coffee they drink in a day, so the store has had to branch out into selling new food items and juice, smoothies, and other items, yet the growth of the past has not returned.

The company has also branched out and started opening stores in Brazil, China, and many countries around the world. Yet growth in these countries brings new costs and risks. Starbucks stock has languished during this time frame, closing at $54.24 on July 2nd, 2015 and three years later, on July 2nd, 2018 the stock closed at $49.06. A Starbucks shareholder who owned the stock during that time frame saw the stock price declined -10.2%, while the S&P 500, which could be owned inexpensively through an index fund, returned +31.2%. There has been a great opportunity cost of owning Starbucks stock during that time frame.

The company is not a bad investment because the stock price has declined. If the company remains solid and the stock price declines, its attractiveness as an investment rises. This doesn't mean that any company becomes more valuable when it's stock price declines, but all things being the same, the margin of safety and potential returns rise as the price declines.

So, the main "take-home" lesson from my foray into concentrated investing is to make sure you understand the business and make sure the CEO responsible for a company's long-term success remains at the company as CEO. If they retire, even if they hand-pick their successor, you should be skeptical about the company's future because the company may change dramatically after their departure. For proof, look no further than General Electric after Jack Welch left and Jeff Immelt became CEO.

That is the lesson I learned with Leucadia National and White Mountains Insurance. I will always consider the departure of the CEO as a reason to keep a watchful eye on the company under the new leader.

An exercise you can use

If you've invested in a company and either the company or its stock has not performed as you'd hoped (and in most cases, let's face it, that just means it hasn't gone up!) then what should you do. The quick and easy answer might seem that you should just sell it, but in these situations, you should be careful not to be a knee-jerk seller or buyer. Remove your emotions from any decision and concentrate your efforts on retesting the assumptions underlying your thesis.

Here's the exercise: use a "clean sheet of paper" framework to determine whether the company's profitability has changed. To use the Starbucks example, if you read through the company's annual report (which you should read every year if you're an investor) you will find a section devoted to the company's financials. Within that section look for the row marked "net income" which is another word for profits. Make sure the company continually increases profits.

Compare the most recent profits with previous years, and make sure the number is growing.

If you see that the company is increasing profits and its fundamentals are good, yet the stock price (the valuation) has stagnated or declined, then it's not necessarily a good idea to sell the stock. That stock might be a good value at a low price, especially if the company is growing.

Read as much as you can to learn about the concerns facing the company and its industry. Ask yourself if the company is in as competitive a position as when you originally bought the stock. If your original thesis has changed and you might decide to sell. Whatever you decide to do, make sure it's based on thoughtful consideration and not a quick decision based on your frustration.

Short-term challenges should not overshadow a strong underlying company. If the company is solid and simply facing a difficult economy or short term unpopularity, it might be well worth it to you to weather the storm. If you have been watching the situation closely, however, and you have noticed a fundamental change in the company, its leadership, or a diminution of its competitive advantage, then it might be time to sell.

The Boiling Frog

The boiling frog is a fable describing a frog being slowly boiled alive. The premise is that if a frog is put suddenly into boiling water, it will jump out, but if the frog is put in tepid water which is then brought to a boil slowly, it will not perceive the danger and will be cooked to death. The story is often used as a metaphor for the inability or unwillingness of people to react to or be aware of sinister threats that arise gradually rather than suddenly.[8]

It turns out that according to modern biologists, the premise is false, and a frog that is gradually heated will change its location as part of its fundamental survival instinct

With investing, however, I think there is a tendency to keep holding stock in a company that has a slowly declining stock price because company fundamentals are deteriorating. The boiling frog metaphor does apply to some extent because you will hold the stock much longer than was "healthy." As investors, we get attached to the idea that our initial reason for buying the stock must still be good. We want to be right, and we get attached to that original investing premise even if things are slowly getting worse.

Put another way, things don't change overnight at a company. There is no "signal" that suddenly you should sell your stock. Instead, things slowly get worse, and while initially you might feel like you're being patient, eventually you might sense you're being stubborn. It's a hard call to make, because in many cases a bit of patience is all that's needed.

In my situation, especially as it relates to Leucadia National, I should have paid close attention to what was really happening at the company, and not what I hoped might happen soon. The leadership was deteriorating over the years, yet the corporate compensation was increasing.

Instead of running for the exits, I held my shares, not wanting to "sell low." I'm certain that I was encouraged by the new CEO, Richard Handler, who expressed optimism that the post-merger future looked bright. Many CEOs, it turns out, are overly optimistic about their abilities to change companies.

Believing the turnaround story, coupled with wanting (and believing) the company would soon turn around, caused me to hold the stock much longer than I should have. Learn from my experience if you can, and when a company faces hard times — whether due to poor leadership or a changing business environment — you may want to consider selling the stock.

I am not alone; Warren Buffett has spoken and written about how after he sunk a lot of money into a dying textile mill called Berkshire Hathaway. The textile business was deteriorating, but rather than closing the mills Buffett continued to try to save a dying business. He says that what he should have done was when he wanted to buy a good insurance company, he should have bought it for a new entity.[9]

"So initially, it was all textile assets that weren't any good. And then, gradually, we built more things on to it. But always, we were carrying this anchor. And for 20 years, I fought the textile business before I gave up. Instead of putting that money into the textile business originally, [had] we just started out with the insurance company, Berkshire would be worth twice as much as it is now."

— WARREN BUFFETT

The take-home message is that if Warren Buffett can stay invested in a business that loses money — and not have the sense to sell it and move on — then anyone is vulnerable to this kind of misjudgment. It makes a lot of sense to remain as objective as possible, and never let your emotions cloud your investment decisions. Ask yourself, "If I can start over today, knowing what I know now, is this a wise investment?" If it is, then you're all set, but if not, you may want to ask yourself why you own the stock if your money could be better invested elsewhere.

25

A CALM CAPTAIN

Think of yourself as the captain of a ship in a storm. As an investor, you will find some days are sunny and warm, and others are stormy and cold. You want to be like a calm captain. Steer the ship through the waves, the wind, and the torrential rain. Keep your eyes focused on where you're going and don't be distracted by the strong gusts and the ocean's salt spray across your face.

Many people get frightened when markets decline. They panic when prices start to decline and markets fall abruptly all around them. This crowd behavior to get fearful permeates markets causing further selling and price declines. What starts like small waves soon turns into tsunamis of terror. It's an uncommon investor who can stay calm under pressure.

There is a reason that Sully Sullenberger landed his US Airways flight on the Hudson River in 2009. He was prepared after the plane was disabled by striking a flock of Canada Geese immediately after takeoff; all 155 people aboard survived.[1]

He was mentally prepared that day and landed the plane calmly. Keep his calm presence in mind as an investor and you'll do well. The key is to invest in great companies and hold them through thick and thin. Don't worry if the markets decline.

Shortly after takeoff, after the plane struck the flock of geese, it lost power in both engines. Sullenberger quickly determined he would be unable to reach any airport, so he piloted the plane to a water landing on the Hudson River. All aboard were rescued by nearby boats.

Sullenberger, described by friends as "shy and reticent," was noted for his poise and calm during the crisis; the mayor of New York, Michael Bloomberg, dubbed him "Captain Cool." Despite the facade of calm, Sullenberger suffered symptoms of post-traumatic stress disorder in the subsequent weeks, including sleeplessness and flash-backs. He said that the moments before the ditching were "the worst sickening, pit-of-your-stomach, falling-through-the-floor feeling" that he had ever experienced. He also said: "One way of looking at this might be that for 42 years, I've been making small, regular deposits in this bank of experience, education, and training. And on January 15, the balance was sufficient so that I could make a very large withdrawal."

As an investor, you will never encounter the kind serious life-or-death experience that Captain Sullenberger experienced. You will not have 155 lives in your hands, nor the responsibility of landing a huge plane on water. However, you can learn to handle the unex-pected with equanimity. No matter how bad things seem in investing (or any aspect of life) you will do best when you keep calm and only take care of things that are within your control.

Every investing environment is different, but you should be indif-ferent to the noise around you. I'm not suggesting that you ignore current events, market news, or what's going on in the world. On the contrary, you should be as well-informed as possible. Yet the tendency for most people is to feel the need to act, and they usually do the wrong thing at precisely the wrong time. This translates to buying when everybody else is greedy and prices are high, and selling when everybody is fearful and prices are low. That is because most people conform to the behavior of the crowd; it's likely an evolu-tionary behavior that historically serves populations well.

The current situation is not constant. Remember that and be

prepared for change. For example, as I write this book the market is in the ninth consecutive year of a bull market in stocks. Many new investors have only seen stocks go up in value, and their friends and family become wealthier with each passing day, week, month, and year. So the human brain kind of projects this to continue forever.

As you read this you may be in the midst of the same bull market, and you may not know how you will react when markets decline. The best policy is usually to do nothing. If you have been thoughtful in your selection process and own great companies, then you don't need to do anything just because the market drops.

It is also possible that the bull market in stocks has changed since this book was written, and the investing landscape is different: stock prices have declined for days, weeks, months, or even years. If that's the case, there is still no need to change your stock holdings as long as the individual companies behind those stocks are still solid.

You can still use the same filtering system to choose stocks, and you may even find that if markets have declined considerably many of the stocks you understand are selling at low prices. This is often because other investors are fearful of buying stocks, and are afraid of the stock market in general. If there is a company you want to own long term, a bear market often provides the low prices that make for extremely successful long-term investments.

The best approach is to keep calm, hold stocks in great companies, and even consider adding to your positions as long as nothing has deteriorated financially with the companies that interest you. Avoid sudden portfolio movements, prize sloth-like inaction, and realize that when people act emotionally they usually make bad decisions.

Keep in mind the image of the calm captain, whether on a ship at sea or flying a plane, with your hand firmly on the wheel and the eyes on the horizon despite the chaos swirling around you.

26

IF

"The record shows the advantage of a peculiar mindset – not seeking action for its own sake, but instead combining extreme patience with extreme decisiveness."

— CHARLIE MUNGER

On the morning after Donald Trump was elected in the 2016 presidential election, the Dow Jones Industrial Average[1] quickly dropped by 800 points. Stock markets hate uncertainty, and when investors panicked the stock market had a short-lived "mini-crash." For those investors prepared to buy stock and unaffected by the fear roiling markets, this momentary dip provided an excellent buying opportunity.

I talked with a friend on the phone a few days later — after markets had rebounded from the crash. My friend told me he *knew* that stock markets would plunge if Trump won the election, and he could have made a killing if he'd had cash on hand to buy stocks.

"If I had money to invest right now. I'd buy stocks and do great because

this reaction is temporary." He was right, but he didn't have the cash and didn't act on his good idea. The key was to *have* the money, *decide what to buy*, and then *take action*.

IF is the important word. This anecdote encapsulates the key to investing success. You have to have money, be prepared, and act decisively. For most people (who never invest), there is always an *IF*: "*If* I had cash," or "*If* I'd started investing when I was young," In every missed opportunity there is an *if* that could have been replaced by planning and action. Preparation and decisiveness are everything in investing.

My friend intellectually understood the huge opportunity that the post-election panic provided, but he did nothing to prepare for it. It is worthless to know things and not act on them. There are so many people on the sidelines of life that can tell you what works and what doesn't. The people who get ahead prepare and act.

Just the other day another friend told me that she has money sitting in cash in her IRA. She has intended to invest it in stocks, but she's waiting until the market crashes to "buy cheap." She told me that she's been waiting for this opportunity for the past three years. She admitted, "If I had just put that money into stocks, they would have gone up over the past three years." She had the cash she needed but never invested it. The confusing aspect about her situation is that she's fascinated with investing and listens to a personal finance podcast every day.

Looking at these two friends, one in the first example with no cash but a good idea, and the second with cash but no clear plan that helps her to invest the money she has.

To avoid saying "*IF only*" as an investor, keep in mind that successful investors:

1. Save money
2. Start investing now rather than try to time the market
3. Have cash available when the inevitable crash occurs

Investing can be simple to those who follow these guidelines.

I'll share a personal story: I wanted to buy Berkshire Hathaway stock in 2015. It had been selling around $150 a share in February, and I noticed it dipped down into the $140 range in June. I waited through the summer and the price continued to decline to the $130 per share territory around Thanksgiving.

I still had the patience and wanted to just wait to see if market volatility would make the stock cheaper. Berkshire was a great company, but I knew market fear could cause the stock to get cheaper.

I got my chance when the stock price declined to $125 a share. I was not paying too much attention to the economic or political factors making the price decline, I just knew a lot about the company and admire Warren Buffett's leadership, so when the price declined to $125 a share I took all the cash I had and bought a bundle of shares.

I think you should realize that sometimes news stories can make a reader fearful in the moment and cause investors to panic and sell shares. Those times of maximum fear is when you want to think about buying.

Here's a quote from one newspaper account that gives you an example of fearful market commentary. I didn't let it affect me because I was not paying attention to the journalist's commentary, I was just keeping my eye on the stock price and looking for a sensible price.

"January got off on a terrible note, with panic about the slowdown in China and crashing oil prices sending the Dow to its worst 10-day start to a year on record going back to 1897.

"Gut-wrenching drama" is how Peter Kenny, a veteran of turmoil on Wall Street, describes it. The independent market strategist pointed to "extreme fear" about the meltdown in oil prices and plunging stock prices in China."[2]

It was an easy decision to make. I had some cash, I knew the company, and I made the purchase. I haven't sold a single share in the years since and the company continues to grow. In my experience, this is the best way to invest: buy shares in quality companies you understand when they are cheap and just sit back and wait. Time is a friend of a great business, and once you buy the stock you don't have to make any more decisions.

"If you buy something because it's undervalued, then you have to think about selling it when it approaches your calculation of its intrinsic value. That's hard. But if you buy a few great companies, then you can sit on your ass. That's a good thing.

We're partial to putting out large amounts of money where we won't have to make another decision."

— *CHARLIE MUNGER*

Prepare to buy stocks ahead of time. Have cash, understand a few great companies, and wait until the market gives you an attractive price.

27

THE ANTIFRAGILE INVESTOR

"Antifragility is beyond resilience or robustness. The resilient resists shocks and stays the same; the antifragile gets better."

— NASSIM NICHOLAS TALEB

A ntifragile things benefit when exposed to shocks. They get stronger when they encounter stressors, volatility, or randomness. Every investor should envision how their stocks will withstand inevitable market crashes.

The point is not merely to survive the market declines when they happen, but to take advantage of the randomness and disorder so that you can buy stocks that are cheap and will emerge from the chaos stronger than when it arrived.

In his book "Antifragile,"[1] Nassim Nicholas Taleb introduces the theory of antifragility this way: "Some things benefit from shocks; they thrive and grow when exposed to volatility, randomness, disorder, and stressors and love adventure, risk, and uncertainty. Yet, despite the ubiquity of the phenomenon, there is no word for the exact opposite of fragile. Let us call it antifragile. Antifragility is beyond resilience or robustness. The resilient resists shocks and stays the same; the antifragile gets better."

There is a *tremendous* opportunity for any investor who uses an antifragile approach and invests cash at opportune times. As Buffett says, "Predicting rain doesn't count. Building arks does." You have to be ready when the storm hits.

Nobody can tell you exactly what to do to become antifragile. The very nature of random events means you can't prepare for them.

Here are a few ideas that you might find useful. Read and think about them and you may find ways to tweak them to make them useful for your own investing.

Barbells: keeping things separate

The first thing is the idea of "an antifragile balance," the idea of two extremes kept separate, with nothing in the middle.

This flies in the face of conventional wisdom that says you should have a well-diversified portfolio of stocks, bonds, cash, etc. It always seemed silly to me to have some money in cash, some in bonds yielding 3%, some yielding 4%, some yielding 5%, and the rest in stocks. This approach seems limited to me because it guarantees mediocre results. After all, you're locking in "safe" returns and limiting your upside but you prevent yourself from having massive upside that you might get with risky investments.

The barbell strategy is an antifragile strategy where you play it very safe in some areas and take risks in other areas. Yet you avoid being "in the middle."

Asset allocation is another way to express this concept. It's another way of expressing the different "buckets" that you might use as containers for your assets.

The financial advising profession formulas that are often touted as "one-size-fits-all" approaches that they recommend to their clients. Just because the idea is fed to you doesn't mean you have to eat it! One formula suggests you should subtract your age from 100 and that is the percent you should invest in stocks (for example, if you're 30 years old, you would invest 100-30 = 70% in stocks and the rest in bonds. As you get older your stock allocation decreases.

I don't think that rules of thumb apply to everyone. If you like formulas and don't want to decide upon your asset allocation, then following an investment formula might be a good idea. However, I think blindly following any investment yardstick benefits an advisor who can use it as a justification from moving you from one asset class to another.

Frequent trading of your account usually benefits the adviser, but it doesn't always help you, the investor. Keep this in mind when you next hear someone talk about the benefits of periodic portfolio rebalancing. Does this make sense or is it mainly busywork to "do something" that may or may not help you in the long term? You should think for yourself and never feel obliged to follow an asset allocation formula.

I agree with the view that an investor should always have a reserve fund set aside for emergencies. It always makes sense to have money that's not invested that you can get your hands on if you ever need it.

Only after you've created a reserve fund for emergencies does it make sense to invest in stocks. In my own investing, I believe I'm in a better position to win with 90% invested in stocks for the long term rather than owning a lot of "safe" bonds whose returns are almost certain not to match those of stocks over the long term.

Another alternative to asset allocation that doesn't follow a financial advisor's formula, but is based on the antifragile barbell approach, is to put a large chunk of your money in a safe investment like cash or a money market account and make some risky or aggressive bets with a small amount.

For example, you could put 90% of your net worth in cash or a money market account, and use the other 10% for extremely aggressive and risky investments. If you invest this way you can never lose more than 10% of your net worth, but you are exposed to a potentially huge upside.

I learned about this approach by learning about Taleb and the concept of antifragility. I don't think it's the best fit for every investor, but it is worth thinking about and it's a good example of the barbell approach where you avoid loading up on assets "in the middle."

While Taleb likes the approach of having the most money in safe investments and a small amount in extremely aggressive and risky investments, Buffett has provided the opposite instructions for cash delivered to a trustee for his wife's benefit. Instead of allocating most of the money in risk-free investments and putting a small amount in stocks, he's flipped it.

Buffett's instructions are for 10% in short-term government bonds and 90% in the S&P 500 index. I find it fascinating to note that both Taleb and Buffett use the barbell approach, even though they invest differently at each end. Buffett's instructions are explained as follows in his will:

"One bequest provides that cash be delivered to a trustee for my wife's benefit...My advice to the trustee could not be more simple: Put 10% of the cash in short-term government bonds and 90% in a very low-cost S&P 500 index fund. (I suggest Vanguard's.) I believe the trust's long-term results from this policy will be superior to those attained by most investors..."

— WARREN BUFFETT

In your thinking, be aware of ways that you can protect your investments through being very safe with a portion of your money, and allow yourself to win big time with riskier bets that could pay off spectacularly.

Examples of antifragility

It's useful to look at other examples of antifragility to prepare the mind for opportunities. Here are a few examples of ways that people can leave the door open to benefit from unexpected events.

A comedian driving uber

One example of antifragility is a comedian who drives Uber as a day job while doing stand-up gigs to further his career on nights and weekends. Another is a technical writer for a software company who writes fiction during her spare time aiming for a bestseller. These risks of becoming a comedian or novelist may be long-shot bets and they are risky, but the costs to participate are low; mainly the time spent pursuing the endeavors.

A snowboarder or surfer

A snowboarder who is accustomed to falling at high speed may become good at falling. Likewise, a surfer may become adept at handling ocean conditions that would be likely to drown a regular person.

The more learning you do, and the more you practice, the better you will be at navigating the slopes and waves of the changing stock market. You don't have to trade often, but you need to get your ramp up your practice. Practice acting quickly and making small experiments with your stock purchases so you can get on a practice groove.

You want to think like an astronaut, athlete, or surgeon who gets a lot of practice, who gets a lot of repetitions under their belt. This will help you develop a sense of intuition about investing; it will become second nature. Just as snowboarder or surfer can withstand shocks, you will similarly be able to "go with the flow" when things get choppy.

Play

Children with the freedom to play gain experience of things such as unfairness, uncertainty, and failure that prepare them for real-world conditions. If adults always step in to correct each unfairness between children, preempt every mistake, and enforce excessive rules, a child may not develop to their full potential.

Damocles, phoenix & hydra

In his book, Taleb uses ancient examples to explain the triad of fragile, robust, and antifragile. Damocles, who dines with a sword dangling over his head, is fragile. A small stress to the string holding the sword will kill him.

The Phoenix, which dies and is reborn from its ashes, is robust. It always returns to the same state when suffering a massive stressor.

But the Hydra demonstrates antifragility. When one head is cut off, two grow back.

Nature

Nature is a recurring demonstration of antifragility. When you lift weights, your body adapts to lift heavier weights next time.

Fragile and antifragile jobs

As an example of an antifragile job, for a bestselling author like Taleb, nothing he can do that generates attention will reduce the sale of his books.

However, if you're a midlevel bank worker and you punch out an annoying drunk in a bar you'll probably get fired, get an arrest record, and become un-hirable. You're extremely fragile.

A taxi driver has more freedom because they are not so dependent on their reputation. Taleb also notes that people who don't seem to care how they dress or look are robust, or antifragile. People who have to wear suits and ties and worry about a bad reputation are fragile.

Buridan's donkey

A donkey that's equally hungry and thirsty and stuck between a bale of hay and water will die of starvation and thirst because it can't decide which to consume first. Yet a random nudge in one direction or the other will solve the problem for him. Randomness helps with decision-making and becoming unstuck. If you try to remove random events then the beneficial stressor disappears. So it's good to have unpredictable events because they push us in new and unexpected directions.

Stoicism

Taleb often talks about stoic principles as ways of handling randomness and becoming antifragile. For example, success can make you fragile, because once you are successful you have much more to lose than you did before. You're afraid of becoming poor. There is a technique called "practicing poverty" that helps reduce your fragility. In essence, you get rid of all the excess things, clothing, and accoutrements of life as a way of preventing yourself from being afraid of losing your wealth.

Develop an antifragile vision

I think it makes sense to prepare for the unexpected. Since we don't know what will happen, as you invest try to avoid the mindset of "how much can I win with this investment?" to one where you ask, "how much can I be harmed if things go wrong?" Just think about stressors as an inevitability and be prepared for the fallout.

A solid start to developing an antifragile vision begins with having cash saved and ready to deploy at the right moment. This means you need immediate access to the money so you can buy something at very good prices when the time presents itself — and you may have only a matter of hours or days.

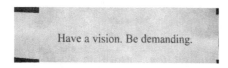

Fortune cookie advice.

The antifragile vision does not require your day-to-day attention. It should keep you motivated and keep you alert to randomness, but most of your time should be spent living your life and doing your work.

Build antifragility into your life and your investing system so it's always running in the background and accessible when needed. You become antifragile by being mindful of what could happen ahead of time and preparing for the inevitable shocks.

If you're fully invested at the top of the market, you'll have nothing to invest at the bottom. People who are "all in" at the market top have the cash to buy at bargain prices later. Warren Buffett's observation rings true when he said, "Only when the tide goes out do you discover who's been swimming naked." All stock investors look brilliant in a bull market. Invest in quality stocks of companies you understand and keep cash available to prepare for when the tide goes out.

An antifragile portfolio

If you want your results to depart from the crowd, you must do things differently

Keep your eyes on as few as 5 stocks, or you can own as many as 20. It is unlikely you will develop a deep understanding of more than 20 companies, but you are in charge of your investments, and if you want to own that many stocks there's nothing wrong with that approach. Just make sure to stay within your "circle of competence" by only investing in companies you understand.

Get decisive when one or a few of those stocks get cheap. Be willing to take a chance investing in a stock you understand, even if you're not 100% sure about it. If you're 70% confident that the company is excellent and the stock selling for a fair (or cheap) price you probably already have enough information to decide to buy. You'll never have perfect knowledge about anything, so there is no point in waiting until your 100% sure.

Have cash

The other major aspect of antifragility that cash injects into your portfolio is that if (and when) stock markets decline you have the liquidity of cash to take advantage of volatility. You will be able to profit and be greedy when others are fearful, and in doing you will be able to take risks during exposure to stress in the stock market and your portfolio will be more robust and resilient.

In the last chapter, you'll recall a friend of mine told me he *knew* the stock market would plummet the day after Trumps's victory and would have invested after the Dow Jones Industrial Average fell 800 points *IF* he had some cash available.

The problem was a lack of preparation and decisive action. It is an example of a great idea and poor execution. You don't want to be a wise person who knows the stock market will crash yet does nothing. Knowing but not acting is useless.

My friend said he would have invested *if* he had cash. The uncertainty and possibility of the word "IF" is embedded in the word "antIFragile."

Having cash on hand, preparing yourself by knowing which stocks you would buy if markets crashed, and being able to deploy cash by buying stocks when conditions present themselves will enable you to become stronger and more robust when the inevitable volatility strikes.

28

CHEAP STOCK TRADES

Apollo 11 landed on the moon when I was one year old. It was a memorable event for many people on earth, no matter what country they lived in or what they believed.

Today Blue Origin and Space X are making reusable vehicles that are reusable so that they can make more trips to space with an operable vehicle that does not need a lot of maintenance between flights. Emphasis is being placed on reusing vehicles otherwise costs get too high. The high costs of the Space Shuttle, which had to be taken apart, inspected and reassembled before each flight is a thing of the past. The shuttle will be replaced by reusable vehicles that can be operated repeatedly at a lower expense.

Stock investing was once expensive

Similar to space travel, stock investing has changed in the past 50 years. Once an activity that was confined mainly to rich people who read the Wall Street Journal, young people who were not rich had no access to stockbrokers. It was simply too expensive to buy stocks, so young people were kept out of stocks.

The high barrier to entry existed because trading technology was expensive, and it was controlled by brokerage firms. The high trading fees investors paid were the brokers' salaries.

Before 1991 it was ridiculously expensive to buy and sell stocks. Just to buy a few shares you had to pay a commission of at least $100, and selling shares cost the same amount. So a round trip of buying and selling stock could cost you more than $200.

Stock Trades Got Cheap in 1991

Everything changed when Etrade began offering online stock trades in 1991.[1]

With the proliferation of online brokerage firms trading became cheap, and with apps like Robinhood and M1 Finance it's free. The barriers to entry have disappeared, and competition among brokerage firms have driven prices down so far that stock trades are now free.

Why Did Trades Get So Cheap?

Stock trades became cheap because of existing infrastructure. The telecommunication network for placing buy and sell orders, which became the backbone of the Internet, was already in place. The funding system for brokerage accounts already existed — in the form of checking accounts. The smartphone was the final piece of the puzzle that lowered the bar, and made it so anyone with a thumb and an Internet connection could trade stocks.

The Internet also made researching companies, learning about stocks, and ordering annual reports as easy as pie. You don't have to go to the library or order annual reports from the company.

Along with cheap trades, the Internet has made stock research (available previously to brokers or through a trip to the library) has become easier than ever. You can Google financial data for any company and get annual reports in a few clicks.

No heavy lifting helped Amazon grow

"I've witnessed this incredible thing happen on the Internet over the last two decades," Jeff Bezos said. "I started Amazon in my garage 24 years ago — drove packages to the post office myself. Today we have 600,000-plus people, millions and millions of customers, a very large company.

"How did that happen in such a short period of time? It happened because we didn't have to do any of the heavy lifting. All of the heavy-lifting infrastructure was already in place for it. There was already a telecommunication network, which became the backbone of the Internet. There was already a payment system — it was called the credit card. There was already a transportation network called the US Postal Service, and Royal Mail, and Deutsche Post, all over the world, that could deliver our packages. We didn't have to build any of that heavy infrastructure."

— JEFF BEZOS

Are cheap trades good for you?

Early on I thought cheap (or free) trades were a bad thing because they make it easy to trade quickly. My learning about investing has always emphasized the importance of concentrating on one company at a time.

But the times have changed, and just because something is fast and easy does not mean it's bad for you. I felt that cheap stock trades hurt investors for a few reasons.

1. With cheap trades, investors may spend less time researching companies.

2. Investors pay higher taxes on any gains held less than one year.
3. Investors pay commissions for every trade.

The first two items are within investors' control; just because trades are cheap does not mean you have to make them, and a patient investor can hold stocks longer if desired. The third item, trading commissions, disappeared when most brokerage firms began to offer commission-free trades in 2019. Free trades and easy access to company information are tremendous advantages for the small investor.

29

ROBINHOOD DREAMS

What is Robinhood?

For readers who have not yet heard of Robinhood, it's an app that provides commission-free stock trading on an iPhone or Android device. It allows you to buy or sell stocks for free and features an easy-to-use interface that lets you keep track of your stock holding and see cutting-edge graphics visualizations of their price movements over various periods. Robinhood gives small investors many of the tools and information sources that used to only be available to wealthy or institutional investors.

Smartphone apps like Robinhood and MI Finance have made it easy to trade stocks largely because the Internet has simplified online trading and electronic payments make it easy to connect brokerage and bank accounts.

In the past setting up a brokerage account took a week or two because you had to fill out forms to open the account and mail paperwork to the brokerage firm. Now the application is completed in minutes without paper.

Why Consider Robinhood?

I think Robinhood makes sense because it simplifies investing. While other brokerage firms have longer track records, if the product is simple it may encourage those who have never invested to get started. I have not personally used Robinhood because I already have a brokerage account, and I don't need another account right now.

However, I think a phone app that allows stock trades is potentially useful to others. I have admired Robinhood's[1] user interface and the way the charts and graphs appear on the app. I have also seen how simple it is to buy a stock; a purchase can be made in just a few moments.

Many other online brokers like Fidelity, TD Ameritrade, and Schwab also have convenient phone apps, and I think readers might want to download and browse the apps (which is possible without actually funding the account) to see if using a phone app makes sense to you.

Experimental, new & exciting

Here's why I think using Robinhood could be a good way for people to start investing. One of Benjamin Graham's[2] student said, "He was innovative, it was a new approach. Everything was experimental. Everything was new. Everything was exciting."[3]

I believe your investing experience should be equally experimental, new and exciting, and any application or device that encourages "creative play" that leads investors to discover the experimental, new, and exciting qualities of investing. If you have not yet tried it (I have only seen Robinhood demonstrated in YouTube videos) one of the most exciting components of the app is the way you can see your stock prices in "real-time" and you can track your returns over the past week, month, three months, year, and since purchase. It automatically calculates your returns and shows you using a dynamic visualization.

Practicing with Robinhood can help improve your investing and help you notice connections you might otherwise not see. I have no way to prove this at the moment, but I do not see any downsides to free and instant stock trading compared to previous methods of buying stock.

In some ways, I think of Robinhood as an airplane flight simulator because the app provides a visual representation of the stocks you own and also a dynamic visualization of their returns over time. The ease of use and visualizations that Robinhood provides might encourage experimentation that could lead to better investment understanding.

I dream about buying stocks using Robinhood. I even watch YouTube videos where other people show their accounts, what they invest in, and how their portfolios are doing. I don't yet have an account, but if stock prices decline sometime soon, I may open an account. I already have a brokerage account with Vanguard, and that firm has recently begun to offer commission-free trades as well, so I see no hurry to start a Robinhood account. However, for those of you who are interested in setting one up, I understand that setting up a Robinhood account is easy to do on your smartphone. Here are the steps:

1. Download the Robinhood app
2. Link the app with your bank account
3. Buy stocks of companies that you understand

The benefit of practice

We are lucky to live in the age of technology because stock investing has become cheap and accessible to the masses. I think this presents a useful proposition to you, the investor who has a smartphone and the willingness to profit from the new technology that makes trading easy to do and inexpensive.

What is the one thing you can do cheaply and easily now that you couldn't before? Practice! It's what any athlete, musician, or artist does to build their skills. There is absolutely no way that an Olympic skater can perfect a triple pike, or a cellist can master a 9/16 time signature in a symphony without hours of practice.

Until now investing was something that was not impossible, but very expensive to practice. You had to have at least $100 to buy stock, and if you made a mistake then selling the stock cost another $100. The penalty for any errors was high, and truly only the rich, or relatively wealthy could dabble in stocks.

Current technology has lowered the bar dramatically so that anyone with a phone, Internet connection, and bank account can participate for free. Though I mention Robinhood in this book, I am aware that MI Finance and a host of other startup brokerage companies also offer commission-free trading platforms.

Whereas in the past investors either had to have a lot of money to spend on brokerage commissions to practice, today people can practice buying with actual stocks. When stock trading was more expensive, it forced investors to think a lot more and spend time with conceptual exercises. It's never a bad idea to think, but going back to the example of an athlete or musician, any endeavor where you can get practice in a real environment (or simulation) will help you improve your skills. This is why all commercial airline pilots must train using flight simulators — to make sure they have adequate "practice" and experience with situations they might encounter in actual flights.

Seeing is believing

I believe you can learn some of the most important investing lessons by using Robinhood or any app you use that facilitates stock investment. History proves that when your money is invested in stocks in the long run your money gains compound interest.[4] Compounding begins when you start investing, and I believe that any app that helps you start investing will *show* you the reality of compound interest. Seeing is believing, and I believe *seeing* your account grow will help you much more than being told that compound interest exists, is good for you, etc.

The other important lesson to learn is to avoid debt, especially the high-interest variety like credit card debt. Any credit card debt is the *opposite* of compound interest. It erodes the value of your money. Those are two of the most important financial lessons anyone can learn. Take advantage of compound interest and avoid debt.

I believe that easy access to the stock markets through free apps provide investors with access to markets they may never have used before, and with the chance to observe for themselves the evidence of compound interest. These apps make practice possible.

30

EQUANIMITY

E quanimity is the key to investing success. It's characterized by your ability to keep cool under pressure. If you can control your temperament you will greatly improve your chances of success.

You should aim to buy stock in great companies and hold them for years. At least 5 years, and preferably 10, 20, 30 years or forever. The other approaches to so-called "investing," namely day trading, speculating on stock options, or trying to predict future price movements are all forms of gambling. You should allow your money to compound over time with few interruptions.

Warren Buffett and Charlie Munger believe that the passage of time is the friend of the investor or business person and impatience his or her enemy. When asked how much he worries about a big drop in the value of Berkshire Hathaway's stock, Munger said succinctly:

"Zero. This is the third time Warren and I have seen our holdings in Berkshire Hathaway go down, top tick to bottom tick, by 50%. I think it's in the nature of long term shareholding of the normal

vicissitudes of worldly outcomes of markets that the long-term holder has his quoted value of his stocks go down by say 50%.

"In fact, you can argue that if you're not willing to react with equanimity to a market price decline of 50% two or three times a century you're not fit to be a common shareholder and you deserve the mediocre result you're going to get compared to the people who do have the temperament, who can be more philosophical about these market fluctuations."

— CHARLIE MUNGER

Aim to stay calm despite stock market storms. Just because the market is climbing or dropping does not mean you need to do anything. Most other people will feel these urges, but just because they're clueless doesn't mean you have to be. The benefit of markets crashing is that you can take advantage of low prices in stocks that you want to buy. Equanimity will help you keep your head when everyone around you is losing theirs.

In the 2017 Berkshire Hathaway Annual Report, Buffett wrote that it makes no sense to use borrowed money to own stocks. "There is simply no telling how far stocks can fall in a short period," he said. "Even if your borrowings are small and your positions aren't immediately threatened by the plunging market, your mind may well become rattled by scary headlines and breathless commentary. And an unsettled mind will not make good decisions," Buffett said.

Speaking of the volatility of markets, and the importance of maintaining equanimity, Buffett said:

"In the next 53 years, our shares (and others) will experience declines...No one can tell you when these will happen. The light can at any time go from green to red without passing at yellow," Buffett said. "When major declines occur, however, they offer extraordinary opportunities to those who are not handicapped by debt. That's the time to heed these lines from Kipling's *If*:

If you can keep your head when all about you are
    losing theirs ...
If you can wait and not be tired by waiting ...
If you can think — and not make thoughts your aim ...
If you can trust yourself when all men doubt you ...
Yours is the Earth and everything that's in it.

I do not doubt that if you invest for more than two or three years you will experience market declines of some sort. No matter what happens, always aim to remain business-like. Keep your wits about you and make decisions with a calm mind.

31

PATIENCE

As an investor, once you own stocks the best plan is usually to do nothing. Inaction is the best plan because when you act, especially based on emotion, you're usually wrong.

Warren Buffett compared his company's investment style to a sloth in a shareholder letter where he wrote, "Lethargy bordering on sloth remains the cornerstone of our investment style. This year we neither bought nor sold a share of five of our six major holdings."[1]

Patience matters because it is not always a good time to buy stocks. When prices seem very expensive, and a bubble might be forming, you can be much better off waiting until prices become more sensible.

There are times when stocks are popular, expensive, and everybody and their cousin are buying them. Just because other people are doing stupid things doesn't mean you have to participate. Buying when everyone else is following the crowd is never a good idea because stocks are often priced too high. It's better to wait until after a market decline, of at least 10% or more.

Nobody is going to keep you from buying, but your future returns will lower if you buy stocks when they are expensive. All things being equal, if you buy stocks cheaply you have a better chance of higher returns. So keep in mind the value of being patient when others are freaking out. Try to think contrary to the crowd and realize that acting like a sloth, moving slowly when everybody is running around like crazy, is often the best path.

Remain patient while you learn, read, and prepare to act when you gather enough information to make a good decision, and eventually, the market will change (it always does) and you'll be more clear about the stock you want to buy at a sensible price.

When to sell a stock

There are times when patience is not rewarded. In his book, Common Stocks and Uncommon Profits,[2] Philip Fisher outlines his three rules for selling a stock:

1. Wrong Facts: There are times after an investor purchases a stock that they realize that the facts do not support their original premise. If the purchase thesis was initially built on a shaky foundation, then the shares should be sold.
2. Changing Facts: The facts of the original purchase may have been deemed correct, but facts can change negatively over time. Management deterioration and/or the exhaustion of growth opportunities are a few reasons why a stock should be sold according to Fisher.
3. Scarcity of Cash: If there is a shortage of cash available, and if a unique opportunity presents itself, then Fisher advises the sale of other securities to fund the purchase.

Sometimes it's difficult to sell a stock because on some level it forces you to admit that you made a mistake when you bought it. You should keep in mind that when you bought, your decision was probably a good decision based on everything you knew then. Perhaps now you have new information about the company, or the management or business has changed. Whatever the reason, if you got the facts wrong when you invested, or they changed, or you need the cash, these are all valid reasons to sell.

In most areas of investing your patience will be rewarded, but I have found that when it comes to selling it's best to act early based on one of the above items. Waiting and hoping that things will change is rarely a successful strategy, at least in my own experience, and eventually, when you sell your stock you'll ask yourself, "Why didn't I do this sooner?" At least that is my experience; every stock I've sold I wish I had made the decision earlier.

32

DECISIVENESS

I f you're just getting started with investing you will be better prepared by spending time learning and not being too active. Warren Buffett said, "Lethargy, bordering on sloth, should remain the cornerstone of an investment style." He also said that "You only have to do a very few things right in your life so long as you don't do too many things wrong."

Charlie Munger says that instead of being constantly in motion, it's best to spend time preparing for opportunity.

"Experience tends to confirm a long-held notion that being prepared, on a few occasions in a lifetime, to act promptly in scale, in doing some simple and logical thing, will often dramatically improve the financial results of that lifetime. A few major opportunities, clearly recognizable as such, will usually come to one who continuously searches and waits, with a curious mind that loves diagnosis involving multiple variables. And then all that is required is a willingness to bet heavily when the odds are extremely favorable, using resources available as a result of prudence and patience in the past."

My greatest personal investing mistakes have been errors of omission — of not making a quality, high-velocity decision on a stock like Adobe or Amazon that I understood well. I've learned that I should adopt a better decision-making process. In the past, instead of buying Adobe and Amazon, for example, I bought the stocks in three other companies I knew less well, mainly because I saw them as "good stocks to invest in" but they weren't companies I understood.

Adobe and Amazon have grown at an astonishing rate, and I should have understood their competitive positions in their respective markets because I buy from Amazon every week and I use Adobe Photoshop almost every in my photography business. It was an error of omission not to buy either of these stocks years ago.

The other mistake I have made on at least three occasions is being too decisive about stocks I did not completely understand. I was investing more in the hope that the stock price would go up, and my confidence based on the "jockeys" running these companies.

It turns out that the businesses had extraordinary histories, and the CEOs responsible for the previously strong performance would retire soon after I bought the stock. This has been my experience twice, and I now view the departure of an extraordinary CEO as a red flag. As Buffett says, "When a management with a reputation for brilliance tackles a business with a reputation for bad economics, it is the reputation of the business that remains intact."

You will only regret being decisive when you buy struggling companies or those you don't understand. I could have improved my results by investing in companies I understand as a customer - companies like and understand. The list of companies I understand includes Adobe, Amazon, Apple, Berkshire Hathaway, Google, and Starbucks plus a few others. I use their products and services and my understanding is based on direct experience. You will have your list of companies, and when you have the money and the price is sensible, decisive action will serve you well.

33

PRICE IS WHAT YOU PAY

"Price is what you pay, value is what you get."

— WARREN BUFFETT

Price is different from value. Sometimes you can pay way too much for something, and other times you can get it on sale.

You want to be sensible when it comes to deciding on the price you pay when you buy anything, especially stocks.

As an investor, you want to aim to pay a price that is roughly equal to or below the value of the company you're buying on a per-share basis. Avoid situations where the price you pay exceeds the value of what you get.

Example of a holiday mug

I'll show you an example of a beautiful and fancy coffee mug that I saw for sale at Starbucks right before the holidays. I knew a friend who I knew would love that mug.

So I wanted to get that mug for my friend, but when I flipped it over it said it cost $25. Keep in mind, this is in the week before Christmas when gift items are selling at their most expensive prices for the year. I passed on buying that mug and left it on the shelf because I knew the value for that mug was less than $25. I had a feeling, that's all, that a piece of ceramic, mass-produced in a factory in China, was not even worth 1/2 of the $25. In simple terms, I estimated that mug was selling for at least twice what it was worth.

Now two weeks later, in early January I happened to stop by that Starbucks and noticed the same mug on sale for $9.99. The value had not changed one iota, yet the price of the mug was 60% less because I was patient and waited a couple of weeks.

While the value remained constant, the price fluctuated wildly. Remember the quote that begins this chapter: "Price is what you pay, but value is what you get." Sometimes price and value converge, and what you pay equals what you get, but at other times price and value can vary greatly.

The mug example explains value investing in a nutshell: you want to avoid buying $9.99 mugs for $25 when. Even if everyone else is buying them at inflated prices, you want to remain patient and take advantage of the times they go on sale, as these opportunities provide terrific opportunities for the prepared investor.

The stock market is there to serve you, but not to instruct you. Just as you should not let the price tag on a mug suggest the value of the item, you should not assume that the stock price reflects the value of a stock. As Ben Graham said, "Mr. Market is there to serve you, not to guide you." Figure out the stock you want to buy first, and do some research to figure out what it is worth. Then be patient and let the market serve you a sensible price.

Take advantage of market fluctuations

There will be times that you can buy the same value (a share of a company you admire) but it will be priced to perfection selling on market optimism way above what you think it's worth. At other times the market will be pessimistic, and that stock will be priced way below what you think it's worth.

Once you have identified a company that you understand and it passes the PALMS filters, figure out a price that seems to "make sense" to you, and be patient if the current market quote is more expensive. From time to time markets tend to fluctuate, and the intelligent investor is patient when stock prices are high and takes advantage of low prices occasionally provided by market fluctuations.

The intelligent investor does not get caught up in the optimism of a bull market, nor the pessimism of a bear market. They simply ignore the former and take advantage of low prices produced by the latter.

I hope the distinction between price and value makes sense to you. Once you see the distinction you will have a new tool in your kit, and you'll be aware of the distinction and ask yourself, "Does the price of this stock accurately reflect the company's underlying value?"

34

YOUR INNER SCORECARD

"The big question about how people behave is whether they've got an Inner Scorecard or an Outer Scorecard. It helps if you can be satisfied with an Inner Scorecard."

— *WARREN BUFFETT*

The inner scorecard

A crucial part of independent thought relates to how we rate ourselves. Warren Buffett refers to this as an "inner scorecard, based on the idea that "A lot of what people do is driven by the quest for admiration from our peers."[1]

Humans tend to act that we feel praise and adulation for our looks, our expertise, our money, or our skills. The trait we are admired for matters less than the admiration itself. The admiration is the token we dance for. We feel envy when others are getting more tokens than us, and we pity ourselves when we're not getting any.

There's nothing wrong with striving to succeed, working hard, and being productive. Where we go astray is when we start to bend our own rules, cut corners, or compromise ourselves in exchange for admiration.

Buffett explains this idea of the Inner Scorecard in the book, "The Snowball: Warren Buffett and the Business of Life" by Alice Schroeder.[2]

"Lookit. Would you rather be the world's greatest lover, but have everyone think you're the world's worst lover? Or would you rather be the world's worst lover but have everyone think you're the world's greatest lover? Now, that's an interesting question. "Here's another one. If the world couldn't see your results, would you rather be thought of as the world's greatest investor but in reality have the world's worst record? Or be thought of as the world's worst investor when you were actually the best?"

— WARREN BUFFETT

In this passage Buffett describes a key to his success in business, investing, and life; he doesn't care what other people think. Where the admiration of others is like a flame to a moth — irresistible yet not beneficial — Buffett is not drawn to it. He just goes about his business and doesn't give in, because he lives his life according to his Inner Scorecard; he simply doesn't care what others think.

While other people are worrying about what others will think of him, and other measures of conventional success, Buffett seems immune to the pressures that cause others to bend. This is one of the many reasons that he has gained success and held on to it over many decades.

Your own experience as an investor will benefit enormously by thinking for yourself, making decisions because your learning and the information you find make sense, and remembering not to be afraid, and investing when markets have declined and prices are low. These things are not always easy to do, but keep in mind the words of the philosopher Baruch Spinoza who said, "All things excellent are as difficult as they are rare."

35

BUFFETT AND MUNGER'S FILTERS

Charlie Munger and Warren Buffett use four filters to choose select stocks. The four filters below are transcribed from a video in which Munger describes their simple set of ideas.[1]

1. We have to deal in things that we're capable of understanding.
2. Once we're over that filter, we have to have a business with some intrinsic characteristics that give it a durable competitive advantage.
3. Then, of course, we would vastly prefer a management in place with a lot of integrity and talent.
4. And finally, no matter how wonderful it is, it's not worth an infinite price. So we have to have a price that makes sense and gives a margin of safety, given the natural vicissitudes of life.

"That's a very simple set of ideas," Munger said. "And the reason our ideas haven't spread faster is they're too simple. The professional classes can't justify their existence if that's all they have to say. It's all so obvious and so simple, what would they have to do with the rest of the semester?"

36

YOU DON'T NEED A GENIUS I.Q

"To invest successfully does not require a stratospheric IQ, unusual business insights, or inside information. What's needed is a sound intellectual framework for making decisions and the ability to keep emotions from corroding the framework.[1]"

— BENJAMIN GRAHAM

A friend's mother bought stock in Starbucks Corporation yet knew little about investing. Her name is Julie, and she started buying stock in the company 25 years ago when it was still relatively small and in its rapid growth phase. She loved getting coffee there and meeting up with friends and family at Starbucks, and once she became a shareholder she loved going to the annual meetings. Her enthusiasm caused her to buy more stock whenever she could.

One day she told me she was thinking of buying Google stock in the IPO — she was so excited to buy stock in the company, and I think she asked me for my opinion on it. I recall saying I wouldn't buy the stock because I didn't understand technology investing — it was outside of my area of competence. Looking back, I was too conservative. My earlier investing self needed to see proof of success over a long time frame before buying stock. Google had not yet proven itself (before they bought YouTube, and before they monetized their search engine with ads).

Google seemed like a risky investment to me in 2004, but obviously, my mistake was one of omission. I knew enough back in 2004 to realize Google was a dynamic, fast-growing company whose name had already become a verb. I easily knew 70% of the information necessary to make a decision, so I could have just bought a small amount of stock, yet I did nothing.

I'm pretty sure Julie bought Google stock because she liked the company so much. The lesson here is with technology companies, you can't be too risk-averse early on. There is always a time, usually a few years, before Wall Street and everyone else figures out that the company is going to massively successful.

If you bought stock only in the two companies that Julie loved, Starbucks and Google, back in 2004, and held those stocks until the present your returns would have been outstanding: Google returned 1,872% and Starbucks 430%. For the sake of comparison, the S&P 500 index fund returned 151% during the same time frame.

Julie's actual returns were far better than that because she started buying Starbucks stock well before 2004.

You can see that Julie kept things simple. She used no math to make her investment decisions, and they were both terrific investments. The lesson to learn is you can make as few as two investments in your lifetime (and put a lot of money into each), and then you can just sit back. You're paying less in commissions, less to financial advisers, and you're paying less in taxes.

If you feel a strong attraction to a company and use its products or services a lot, that's a good sign; there are likely many other people who feel the way you do. If you're a regular customer you probably know a lot about the company through your own experience that other investors on Wall Street do not yet know. It doesn't take a lot of smarts to be a good investor when you stick to what you understand.

37

ZERO-BASED THINKING

O nce you start investing you may notice one of your stocks is not performing well. For some reason, the story changed from when you bought it. The company may not be earning much money, or the leadership is not innovating fast enough. Maybe the business is losing out to new competition. There are so many reasons that stock prices decline. Your task as an investor is to be like an investigative reporter, and find out why the company is failing, and determine if the problem is temporary and will likely pass, or if it's systemic and it's time for you to sell the stock.

It's not just you. You may feel alone and stuck in a bad investing situation, but many other investors have faced similar conundrums. It's not just you, it's the reality of being a part-owner of a business that sometimes you have to take a good, hard, objective look at what's going on and decide whether you should just sit tight or decide that it's time to make a decision and sell the stock.

In my view, the worst thing you can do is remain frustrated and want to sell, but do nothing instead. If you think feeling these emotions and not making decisions with clarity is just something you're doing, let me remind you that you are not alone. Many people would rather keep driving in the wrong direction instead of acknowledging that they've made a wrong turn. Even great investors hold onto stocks long after the company has changed for the worse. When you recognize this has happened you can just wait things out and hope the situation improves, or you can sell the stock and move on.

I have owned stocks too long on more than one occasion. I can recall five stocks that I thought I would own forever, and my desire to stick with them forever clouded my good judgment and kept me from selling when I should have. When a company has trouble for a year or two in a row, you may be better off selling it instead of hoping things will improve.

It seems that when companies start to struggle for one reason or another (the business deteriorates, the management is incompetent, or both) you are better off just selling. The worst decisions I've made were when I had a bad feeling in my gut about a company that I ignored.

I think the psychology behind this behavior is that when you bought the stock, you thought the company was a great idea (obviously, or you wouldn't have bought it!) Then the company performs worse than you hoped it would, so you either have to sell it (which means admitting to making a bad decision) or to stick with a bad stock hoping things will get better, which they rarely do. It's the triumph of hope over experience.

People in bad relationships make the same type of mistake. There is a feeling that you've already invested so much time and energy, so there is a hesitancy to break up. The time invested in the past clouds decisions about the present. Of course, dealing with the present situation is much healthier than attaching ourselves to the past, but humans tend to cling to feelings or memories in the past. The people and relationships may or may not be available to talk and "work things out," but the possibility to fix things exists.

If a business is financially suffering it is much harder to fix things and move on. Businesses that take a turn for the worse are like The Titanic. They move too slowly to course-correct and wind up sinking. There are more reasons for business failure than I can list, and when bad things start happening it's very hard to fix problems.

As excited as you may have been when the voyage began, you need to be realistic about any changes to the company or how the current business climate may have impaired the business and be ready to jump ship if you think it's sinking.

Try not to be emotional about your investments, although this is extremely difficult because of human emotion. Be as "unemotional" as you can, keep calm, and look carefully to see if there's an easy fix in sight and if management is taking sensible steps to right the wrongs. If not, you may be in for a long and expensive lesson that will eventually teach you a lesson the hard way.

What would you do now?

Here is the question to ask:

"If I were starting over today: what is the best decision to make right now?"

It's a great question because if you own stock and the company or its industry changes, you can feel emotionally stuck. You think about the past and the time and money you wasted and may never get back. You start worrying about what to do. You have to realize that the past is gone. Any mistakes in investing are two-way streets. If you bought something in the past you can sell it today and solve your problem.

What is zero-based thinking?

Dwelling on mistakes and sucking your thumb when you should act will get you nowhere. If you pretend that you're starting new right now you make better decisions for the future. The idea of Zero-based thinking[1] is a decision-making process based on imagining yourself back at the point before particular decisions were made, and free to make those decisions with the knowledge that you have now about their outcome.

Here's a really simple way to use zero-based thinking, and I learned it from Brian Tracy, who suggests that you ask this questions:[2]

"Is there anything that I am doing today, that knowing what I now know, I wouldn't get into today if I had to do it over?"

Tracy calls this a "KWINK" analysis — "Knowing What I Now Know," and he says that in times of rapid change, there are always areas in your personal and business life you wouldn't get into today if you had to do them over. He says your willingness to ask and honestly answer this question is the key to remaining flexible and quick on your feet in times of turbulence."

One aspect of investing that I enjoy is that it encourages you to use your brain in new ways. We are just used to going through life making decisions in many areas of life where it's hard to quantify decisions, and you can go one "feeling" a lot and you'll be alright. But with investing, or any situation where the financial stakes are high, you need to keep your wits about you and not get swept up in emotion.

For example, one thing I've noticed in my own investing, and also the investments of others, is that once you've owned shares of a company for a long time, you may feel nostalgic for it. It's like rooting for a sports team, and the team could be awful, but you're still loyal to the team because you know it well and you've rooted for it for such a long time.

Warren Buffett started buying shares in a money-losing textile mill called Berkshire Hathaway in 1962. He continued buying the stock until he took control of the company, even though his purchases made him the majority owner of a textile business that was failing. Even for a great investor like Buffett, it was hard to admit that the investment in textile mills was a money-losing situation because the textile business was waning and the company's financial situation was failing. In 1985, the last textile operations were shut down.[3]

Warren Buffett occasionally makes investment mistakes, and you can too. It's a good sign that you are able to remain objective and rational about the stocks you own.

Are you already good at removing your emotions from the decision-making process, or is this hard for you? If you just stick with facts then you already have an advantage, but many people have self-doubt and nostalgia that can get in the way. As humans, we are naturally going to make decisions based on our "gut feelings" or because we want something, but just realize that we all share these tendencies.

You can learn to identify when your emotions are negatively impacting your ability to make rational decisions, and remove them from the equation. Professional poker players are a good example of this. To win consistently at poker you have to be able to calculate the odds and use that information to decide when to play and when to fold, but even the best poker players are vulnerable immediately after winning or losing a big hand.

"A big win can make you feel invincible, whereas a large defeat can entice you into chasing your losses. It's called being "on tilt" and its effect is so hard to resist that some players will deliberately fold the hands following a significant game rather than run the risk of making an unwise, emotion-fueled decision."[4]

Similar, but more subtle, situations exist in running a business. We can chase losses or pour money into projects that we should cancel, yet we dilly-dally and hope things might turn things around in the future despite signs to the contrary.

Benefits of zero-based thinking

Zero-based thinking removes everything from a decision except for your clear view of what has already happened in the past, and it helps you make hard choices. Even though it sounds complex, let's take a look at a way that you can put it to work simply.

Let's say you bought a stock many years ago and the company hasn't been growing very well lately. The management isn't doing anything terrific, but they're not failing miserably either. You've been hoping they would turn things around, but it simply hasn't happened yet. You're hoping it bounces back.

Now imagine that at sunset today you have to sell this stock and then rebuy it with no cost whatsoever. No brokerage fee and no hassle. Would you buy back the stock? If you would, then no problem, you're all set and you truly believe in the company.

But, if you'd hesitate when it comes to buying that stock after you were forced to sell it, then you have new information. You probably don't want to own that stock. You're holding onto it for the wrong reason. You are afraid to admit you made a mistake, you're being nostalgic, or you're hoping things will change in the future. These are all pitfalls based on emotion, and they're problems that zero-based thinking can help you avoid.

If you've been investing for a while, then these ideas will probably make sense to you. If you haven't invested in stocks yet, or do not have much experience with them yet, then you're in a good position to learn a lot now. Keep the concept of zero-based thinking in mind and you will find it enormously helpful not only with investment but in many other areas of your life. Just ask yourself, "knowing everything I know now, would I do this again?"

Time spent researching a stock in the past, just as buying the stock and following the company's ups and downs over many years is also a sunk cost. Any mistake you made is history; learn from it, and decide if you would buy a stock today if you had it to do over again. If the answer is "yes," then stick with it. If the answer is "no," then why on earth are you still holding the stock?

The behavioral part of investing is fascinating because it deals with hopes and dreams, with gaining and losing. Understanding how psychology works and being mindful of what we do when we make mistakes — and how we course-correct — is useful. It's also helpful to note if we have a history of not course-correcting when we should. I have had several cases of holding stocks I should have sold earlier, and waiting when I should have just bought. I try to learn from as many mistakes as I can.

Sometimes you just have to realize you made a mistake and start over. It's like when you'd make a drawing or painting and you hated it, so you crumpled it up and started over. I think as we age, and especially commit money to an investment, there's a feeling that we have to salvage everything, that if we put time and money into something we need to extract it all and make everything useful. I think there's some wisdom to recognizing the "sunk costs" of life when you just screwed something up and it's time to start over. Salad in the fridge gives you the sign that it's time to toss it. Milk starts to smell. That bread with the blue-green mold gives you a signal that it's time to toss it in the compost bin.

Stock investments don't give you a visual cue that they no longer make sense and it's time to sell them. It's different for every investor, but I'd say that if the company you've invested in has changed significantly, or its industry has changed and the company is no longer competitive, then it's time to reconsider your position. You have to pay attention to the companies you own. I think the best test is if you have a better opportunity in another stock then just sell your current stock and reinvest it in something with better prospects.

If the company you have invested in is growing at about 6% a year, and you can't see any way that will improve, and you see another company that looks like it could grow at 10% a year, then to me there is an opportunity cost to staying the course. If the new stock passes the PALMS filtering system, it makes sense to pursue a new opportunity to compound your money at a higher rate of return.

In a nutshell

One thing we can learn from our own mistakes, or those of others, is that if you're chasing a loss on your investments, that loss is detracting from future gains. Every year you're stuck owning stock in a failing or middling company you are foregoing gains.

Ask yourself: "If I was not in this situation, knowing what I now know, would I get into it today?"

It's amazing how many people will stay in a bad situation, or continue with a bad course of action, because of their unwillingness or inability to admit that they made a mistake, or that they were wrong in the past.

Remember that when you made the decision, it was probably a good decision based on the situation at that time, but now the situation has changed. Now you have to evaluate your situation based on the current reality.

We can't change the decisions we have made in the past, but we can use everything we've learned in the past to make smart decisions right now that will have a positive effect on our future.

KEEP IT SIMPLE

"If you can't understand it, don't do it."

— *Charlie Munger*

The best things are often the simplest. How this translates with investing is that you keep things simple by not attempting to be extraordinary in areas you have no edge. You have to do a lot of learning, and become intelligent in a variety of different disciplines, but you don't have to invest in them all. With investing, you learn from many different disciplines - math, biology, physics, business, philosophy, technology, and human behavior — and then you try to concentrate your thinking around your best ideas, things you understand well.

"As an investor, you're constantly weighing options," Munger said. "You can't invest in everything, so you have to choose one thing that is way better than the other."

Consider that any time you invest in a stock, you're effectively saying that it is a better use of your money than the hundreds, or thousands of other companies out there.

I like stories that illustrate useful concepts, and one that jumps to mind is a story that Charlie Munger told a large group of investors at the 2019 Daily Journal meeting. Pay special attention to the simple question he asks, and also his surprise that none of the bright people in the audience can answer it.

"Years ago, one of our local investment counseling shops, a very big one, they were looking for a way to get an advantage over other investment counseling shops, and they reasoned as follows: 'We've got all these brilliant young people from Wharton and Harvard and so forth, and they work so hard trying to understand business and market trends and everything else, and if we just ask each one of our most brilliant men for their single best idea, and then created a formula with a collection of best ideas, we would outperform averages by a big amount.'[1]

It seemed plausible to these investment advisers that this would work, because they were ill-educated in the reality of real-life investing. "So they tried it out, and of course it failed utterly," Munger said. "So they tried it again, and it failed utterly, and they tried a third time, and it also failed.

"Of course, what they were looking for is the equivalent of the alchemists of centuries ago who wanted to turn lead into gold. They thought if you could just buy a lot of lead and wave your magic wand over it that would be a good way to make money.

The investment advisors were were looking for the modern equivalent of turning lead into gold, and of course it didn't work. The interesting part of this story is that Munger then asked a very interesting group of people from all over the world to provide an answer to this very simple problem: "Why did that plausible idea fail?" Munger asked. "Think about it a little. You've all been to fancy educational institutions. I'll bet there's hardly one in the audience who knows why that thing failed."

To Munger's surprise, nobody answered his question, prompting his to say:

"That's a pretty ridiculous demonstration I'm making. How can you not know that? But that's one you should be able to answer. *It shows how hard it is to be rational on something very simple.*

"Now, at a place like Berkshire Hathaway or the Daily Journal, we've done better than average. Now there's a question: Why has that happened? And the answer is pretty simple: We tried to do less. We never had the illusion we could just hire a bunch of bright young people and they would know more than anybody about canned soup and aerospace and utilities and so on and so on and so on. We never had that dream. We never thought we could get really useful information on all subjects like Jim Cramer pretends to have.

— CHARLIE MUNGER

Munger explained that he and Buffett always realized that if they worked very hard they could find a few things where they were right and that was a reasonable expectation and enough for investment success[2].

He said that if you asked Warren Buffett the same question that the investment advisors asked, if you just asked him to "Give me your best idea this year" and you just followed Buffett's best idea, "you would find it worked beautifully."

The point is that Buffett's success was based on the fact that he wasn't trying to know the whole universe. He would give you one or two stocks.

In the same way, you can invest better if you have more limited ambitions. The key is not to try and invest in all the stocks out there. Look at one or two stocks at a time, and keep things simple.

Here are a few more quotes from Charlie Munger on sticking to what you know and keeping things simple.

- "Well, opportunity cost is a huge filter in life. If you've got two suitors who are eager to have you, but one is way better than the other, you're going to choose that one rather than the other. That's the way we filter stock buying opportunities. Our ideas are so simple. People keep asking us for mysteries, but all we have are the most elementary ideas."[3]

- "I like people admitting they were complete stupid horses' asses. I know I'll perform better if I rub my nose in my mistakes. This is a wonderful trick to learn."[4]
- "Forgetting your mistakes is a terrible error if you are trying to improve your cognition."[5]
- "There's no way that you can live an adequate life without many mistakes," Munger said. "In fact, one trick in life is to get so you can handle mistakes. Failure to handle psychological denial is a common way for people to go broke."[6]
- "You don't have to be a genius to be a good investor; just avoid doing stupid things. Just say "no" to any investment you don't understand. It's very simple, but that's why most people ignore it. They get excited about the next hot stock, something that's been growing super fast. Yet they don't understand it and it blows up, and they're left holding the ashes."

One of the reasons that the PALMS filtering system works is that it's simple enough that anyone can quickly rule out many stocks. For example, if you don't know anything about oil and gas companies, just forget about ever investing in them. By the same token, if you don't know much about banking or insurance companies, rule them out. Just writing down the list of companies *you do understand* eliminates thousands of companies that would be bad investment ideas.

Simplicity is a great tool for investors because things can easily get complicated in a hurry if you try doing too many things. You simply can't achieve the depth of understanding across too many different disciplines. But you can get really good in just a few spots, and as long as you stick to those spots you'll likely do well.

As a professional photographer, I own only a few cameras and lenses. These are the best I could buy, and everything fits into one case. This minimalist approach favors quality of gear over quantity, and it means I can concentrate on the person I'm photographing instead of my equipment.

Because I have a simple collection of cameras, I am familiar with how they work in a variety of situations. So, when I'm behind the camera I have already avoided technical problems that crop up when you have too much equipment, and I can devote my attention to the job at hand.

My approach to camera gear mirrors my approach to investing, because both benefit from simplicity. The intelligent investor stays within their circle of competence, and they consider few stocks. They become so familiar with their stock selecting tools — filters like the PALMS system — that they use them with the same facility of a camera in the hands of a professional photographer.

An investor trains their mind to quickly assess the likelihood of a company having success. They also need to quickly imagine the ways the company could fail. They need tools that help them quickly decide if a stock passes through to the next level to even be considered. The process is not complicated at all, it becomes instinctive.

I think one of the best gifts of the investor is the ability to rule out stocks. Instead of picking out the best stock, just rule out all the stuff you don't understand. Then simplicity works in your favor because you can take a very close look at the few stocks that you actually "get" and you can put them through the filters and figure out which ones make the most sense.

When you start to look at different companies you start to get more familiar with the investment process. It's kind of like playing soccer, tennis, or skiing, or even learning a foreign language. When you begin they seem difficult, and mastery seems far away. But anyone who has stuck with a sport or a language for a few years knows how much easier it becomes with regular practice.

The same goes for investing, and you'll find that the more time you spend at "play" with stocks and using the filters you've learned in this book, the more of an expert you'll become. It's funny, the best investors aren't serious people who bury their heads in books full of numbers all day long. It's true, they read a ton, but they read about all kinds of different subjects, and they have fun, and they are well-rounded people.

The best investors are lifelong learners. The more they learn, the easier their investing becomes. Knowledge tends to compound over time, and everything you learn builds upon itself. Through it all, great investors get even better by keeping things simple by playing the game they understand, and always looking for ways to simplify their process and improve their results.

39

THREE WAYS TO SUCCEED

There are three ways to succeed as an investor. You can succeed intellectually, physically, or emotionally. I have learned this through personal experience, observing other investors, and reading a lot about investing.

Intellectually

The intellectual way is how we all dream of investing. It's being so gifted you just know which stocks to buy. The intellectual way requires insights into companies and the future .

One classic of the intellectual stock investor is Warren Buffett. People like him show up once in a long while, and it's extremely difficult to emulate their success. It's like loving basketball and trying to be the next Michael Jordan; it's a worthy goal, but for most people it's not in the cards.

Physically

The second way to succeed is the physical way — to work harder. You wake up super early and fueled by coffee or Red Bull you start at sunrise and grind away till midnight. You are constantly glued to screens and read transcripts of conference calls. You're watching the blinking red and green symbols and search for divine signals from stock charts like you are reading tea leaves. Then you go home and read more, and you work all weekend too. This is what the analysts on Wall Street do, at least everyone tries it, and claim it works. It must work for some of them — though I can't say for sure. I live in Seattle and I'm far from the hustle and bustle of Wall Street, but I observe a lot of investors and I see that many of them can't beat the averages... because they are the averages. Yet they must think it works, or they wouldn't keep trying so hard.

Emotionally

The third way to succeed as an investor is difficult emotionally. When the market starts to tank, you pay no attention to it, no matter what happens. If it drops 10% you don't fear. If it drops 20% or 25% and the headlines are calling for the end of the economy as we know it, you don't worry.

Ellis says that the emotional way is the only reliable way he knows to succeed as an investor.

> *"I'm not smart enough to succeed the intellectual way, and I can't work hard enough to succeed the physical way. But the emotionally difficult way takes very little time and makes no intellectual or physical demands on you at all. Statistically, judging by how the public invests, most people don't like the emotionally difficult path. Then again, more and more people are trying it; the amount of money in index funds has been rising year after year. The emotional path is the only reliable way that I know of to succeed."*
>
> — CHARLIE ELLIS

I like the challenge of succeeding intellectually. It does not bother me that it is physically demanding to spend so much time reading and watching videos. I don't consider it a job, I consider it a source of enjoyment and learning. \

The emotional path is the easiest way to succeed because it doesn't require intellectual brilliance or many hours devoted to research. You can just commit to investing in index funds at regular intervals over the long term and you'll get a perfectly decent result.

I don't think you have to pick just one path, and in practice I believe that investing is most effective when it blends intellectual, physical, and emotional strengths. It is good to be aware of each quality, and eventually you'll figure out the mix that works best for you.

40

EXPERIMENTAL, NEW AND EXCITING

"He was innovative, it was a new approach. Everything was experimental. Everything was new. Everything was exciting."

— EDWIN SCHLOSS, SPEAKING OF BEN GRAHAM

As you've learned, investing is more than just a bunch of numbers and ratios that, if you look at them long enough, will lead you to good investments. They talk about P/E ratios, Alpha, Beta, and whether a company will hit earnings. They write about shorting stocks and whether or not to buy put or call options. They deal in esoteric symbols of the stocks as derivatives of companies, instead of as the integral "parts" of companies that they represent.

I would guess that while many investors are not creative types, the best investors bring a lot of creativity to their work of looking at companies from all angles; they see things that others miss.

Every investor brings unique skills and understanding of the investment process, and each person has a different temperament as well. Ultimately, it's up to each investor to identify and buy stock of successful businesses. How you learn about these companies and will determine your success, and you'll enjoy it more if your process is experimental, new, and exciting.

PART V

THOUGHT INTO ACTION: PUTTING IT ALL
TOGETHER

41

THOUGHT INTO ACTION

W riting this book has changed the way I invest. It forced me to ask myself why I had been so indecisive about buying stock in Amazon. I had a strong interest in buying that stock many times over the years, but the stock always seemed expensive. Writing this book forced me to reconsider all aspects of Amazon, and realize that the company's many strengths might justify the stock price.

I recently heard an interview with Buffett in which he was asked why he had never purchased Amazon stock. He said he had followed the stock since it was cheap, explaining, "It's a little hard when you look at something at "x" and it sells at 10x to buy it.[1]"

Speaking of Amazon CEO Jeff Bezos, Buffett said, "I was impressed with Jeff early. I never expected he could pull off what he did...on the scale that it happened. At the same time he's shaking up the whole retail world, he's also shaking up the IT world simultaneously. These are powerful, powerful ideas with big potential, and he's executed," Buffett said.

I have been a long-time Amazon customer and have seen the company grow before my eyes in Seattle. It's been a gradual process, and it was not always obvious that Amazon would become profitable, nor that it would become the dominant force in both retailing and cloud computing. When this reality became evident to investors, the stock price had already ascended to $500, then $700, and then $1,000. The stock price always went up.

By fixating on recent stock prices I was doing something called "anchoring,"[2] a psychological phenomenon that Daniel Kahneman describes in his book, "Thinking Fast and Slow[3]." Because I saw Amazon selling for low prices, all subsequent prices seemed expensive. It's the same bias that Buffett refers to when he said, "It's a little hard when you look at something at x and it sells at 10x to buy it."[4]

A behavioral bias can hamper clear decision making if you're not careful. Let me explain why I believe this is so: Amazon stock price has climbed more or less in sync with the company's growth. The question we need to ask is whether the increase in price accurately reflects the company's value, or if the price has climbed too high compared to what the company is worth.

42

DECISIVE ON AMAZON

"Spend each day trying to be a little wiser than you were when you woke up."[1]
— *Charlie Munger*

Throughout this book I have encouraged readers to invest only in companies they are capable of understanding. It makes sense to buy great companies early on when you can buy their shares at a low price and have many years of growth ahead of you.

Amazon is one company I understand well, but I never bought the stock because at first it wasn't profitable, and later it became expensive. I moved to Seattle in 1994, the same year that Jeff Bezos founded Amazon, and I've witnessed the company's torrid growth before my eyes. Like many others, I buy something at Amazon at least once a week, and I use many of the services included in Prime membership.

While Amazon has grown before my eyes, looking back it was not always obvious that Bezos would execute his vision with such success.

One thing I've learned in life and investing is that it's good not to dawdle. Sometimes it's better to just make a decision, even if you don't know everything you wish you knew. The decision may turn out to be wrong, but it's better not to dawdle too much. Based on Amazon's strengths in retailing and cloud computing I decided to put Amazon through the PALMS filter and consider buying the stock.

PALMS FILTERING SYSTEM FOR AMAZON

- Profitable: Yes.
- Adapting to Technology: Yes. Kindle, Amazon Web Services (cloud computing), Alexa, streaming music and video.
- Loyal Customers: Yes. Current customers keep buying. New customers try Amazon Prime and join the company's ecosystem every day.
- Moat to Protect: Yes. A huge and widening moat.
- Sensible Price: Yes.

Sensible price is the only factor I have not been sure about. Every time I look at the price it seems expensive, yet I think the price is not that expensive when you take into account the company's bright future.

Amazon is growing at such a high velocity that the stock price seems high, and constantly going higher. That is why I never bought; my old way of thinking was to buy stocks when they were "cheap," and Amazon stock has never been cheap. But even if the stock has never been cheap, the question remains: "is it sensibly priced?"

Though I can't say with absolute certainty, I'm 70% sure the price is sensible. If I wait until I'm 100% sure, I may never buy this stock.

Throughout this book I have suggested that readers be flexible when determining a sensible price, yet in my own behavior I have been a cautious little squirrel when it comes to Amazon, hoarding my acorns instead of using them to buy stock.

The problem was that I was focused on the price, and based on price alone it always seemed expensive compared to its prices a few years earlier. I was anchored to a past instead of looking at the incredible growth story right before my eyes.

All of these "old" ways of evaluating Amazon's stock prevented me from buying it for many years, but while writing this book I kept reminding myself of how important it is to be flexible on price and not miss out big time. If I could just keep in mind the success the company has had making its vision come to life, then the investing picture would be snap into focus in the long term. The philosopher Spinoza's words came to mind: "You must look at things under the aspect of eternity."

So, I just told myself that no matter what, I would commit to buying Amazon stock by the end of the year. December flew by, and before I knew it, the date was December 29th, 2017. It was the last trading day of the year, and if I wanted to act on my decision to buy Amazon stock I only had a few hours left. I did not know with absolute certainty if the price was sensible, but I had felt this way for years, and I always missed out because it seemed expensive.

On that last trading day of the year, I had about 70% of the information I wished I had about Amazon's price. I knew the company was growing ferociously, and that was enough to make the high-quality, high-velocity decision[2] to buy the stock.

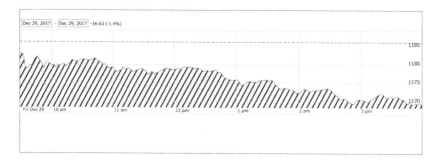

Amazon stock on the day I finally decided to invest.

At the market open on December 29, 2017, Amazon was selling at about $1,180 a share. I noticed the price declining slightly and this continued throughout the day. As I prepared to buy shares, the stock price kept getting cheaper. Since I had already decided to buy shares by the end of the day, I waited to see how low the stock price would go. In the final minutes of the day, I set a buy limit order[3] at $1,169.50. Moments before the market closed, the price declined and my order was filled. After years of admiring the company and being a loyal customer, I had *finally* become an Amazon shareholder. It was an awesome feeling, and somewhat hard to describe. I had hesitated because I thought the stock was too expensive for years. Yet now my filtering system provided a step-by-step way to make a decision.

Time will tell how well the PALMS system worked. Whatever happens in the short term is anyone's guess, but over the next three to five years (and beyond) I believe Amazon will continue to grow, and if it continues to succeed in its mission, Amazon's share price should reflect the company's success.

While writing this book, I learned the importance of being flexible on price as long as a company meets other important investment criteria, and I wanted to follow this advice myself. I wanted to minimize any regret of not buying Amazon; I don't want to look back when I'm 80 years old and say, "Why didn't I buy it? Amazon was a fantastic company. I missed it big time!"

I bought this stock for the long term because I believe that Amazon will become an even more innovative, enormously impressive company in the next 5, 10, 20 years and beyond, and I believe that as the company grows its stock price will follow. A nice side effect of the purchase is that readers now have a "real-life" example of the PALMS filtering system in action.

Something that sets Amazon apart

One thing I have noticed about Amazon that kept me from investing for many years is that they never seemed profitable, and I always used that as a gauge of whether a company made sense as an investment. I still think profitability matters tremendously, but it turns out I simply wasn't seeing what Amazon was doing.

Amazon could have become a profitable company much earlier if that was their goal. Yet, instead of trying to impress investors with profits, they plowed that money back into the company, using it to innovate and to grow the business. So, while the company did not appear to be turning a profit, it would have easy to do. Instead of trying to impress investors with short-term profits, Amazon plowed that money back into the business.

Amazon got a "pass" from Wall Street for years — because they went years, even decades without showing a profit, and investors large and small keep bidding up the stock. I didn't know why until I heard Scott Galloway, a professor at NYU's school of business, describe the phenomenon.[4]

"In the letter that Jeff Bezos sent to his investors in 1997 about investing across three core areas that are non-perishable and making massive investments, was his really compelling vision that he has stayed true to and that they execute against every day.

And as a result, their stock keeps getting bid up, so they're effectively fighting unfair with cheaper capital, and can try 10 things for every three things the other tech companies can try, and every one thing an old economy firm can try. If you play Texas Hold 'Em poker at some point when you hold the most chips, you can muscle everyone else out of the game — that's Amazon."

— SCOTT GALLOWAY

I never thought about Amazon that way, as a company that can muscle others out of the game. That is because I focused less on Amazon's competition and more on what they were doing to delight customers. A by-product of obsessing over customers was punishing their competition who could not touch their selection, customer service, or fast delivery.

I could see more and more people going to Amazon first to search for things they needed to buy. Amazon was becoming a search engine like Google that helped people find a wide variety of products in one place. I also heard the company's name popping up in everyday conversation: "Oh, you need a bluetooth speaker? Why don't you just buy it on Amazon?" or someone exclaiming in delight, "I bought those AA batteries on Amazon yesterday and they arrived today!"

I know people who bought Echo speakers (Alexa devices) and immediately started using them to play music, set timers when cooking, make shopping lists, and ask Alexa to tell them a joke. In addition to all the ways customers were embracing voice technology with their Echo devices, I could see Amazon Web Services (AWS) beginning to dominate cloud computing as Amazon's most profitable subsidiary.

There were so many positive things blooming in Amazon's garden because of the seeds of experimentation planted many years earlier.

Final thoughts on thumb-sucking

I sat around admiring Amazon for years, but I sucked my thumb instead of buying the stock.

None of us are born wise, but the most we can hope for is to get better every day, and in my own investing journey this means learning not to dawdle too much, and to make a decision, even if it's wrong. I realize I can always course-correct later.

Reflecting on Munger's advice to "spend each day trying to be a little wiser than you were when you woke up[5]," I feel that writing this book has forced me to learn to use tools that help me to be more selective and decisive, and I believe that everyone who reads this book can use these tools themselves.

43

AMAZON ONE YEAR LATER

"To invent you have to experiment, and if you know in advance that it's going to work, it's not an experiment."

— JEFF BEZOS

December 2018 Update:

I write to provide readers with an update one year after publishing the first edition of *Stock Market Intelligence*. It's been exactly one year since I wrote about my decision to buy Amazon stock.

At the time, I had no idea that applying the PALMS filtering system to Amazon would work out so well. So far the company continues to fire on all cylinders. I was a little fearful to write this book to teach other people my approach to investing for the simple reason that I had no way to know it would work; the PALMS filtering system was an experiment.

I had hoped my approach would work, and I spent a lot of time developing the system, but in the end, I knew that my action would be recorded in this book, and there was a chance I would fail. It would be hard to retain credibility with readers if they saw I screwed up.

As you'll recall from the last chapter, I invested in Amazon at $1,169.50 on the last trading day of 2017. I decided to apply my filtering system in real life and put it in writing for future readers of this book as a case study in applying my investing method.

I'm glad I bought the stock when I did for two reasons. The first reason is that the company has grown and the stock price has increased. One year is too short a time frame to gauge the success of this system, but fortunately the company has continued to execute with success.

The second reason I'm glad I decided to buy Amazon stock will be instructive to you, this book's reader. I pushed through my fear of buying Amazon stock even though I wasn't 100% sure it would be a great idea. Sometimes you may feel you don't have enough information to be decisive.

I'm glad I decided to buy the stock and it worked out because it shows readers that even the author of a book, or any investor has some trepidation before making a stock purchase. It's good to be bold and have an adventurous attitude instead of always being defensive.

The book started with the quote by Picasso, "I'm always doing things I can't do. That's how I get to do them." That quote means a lot to me because it reminds me to always try new things and experiment. Sometimes things won't work out the way I want, but I always pick failure's pocket and try to learn something along the way.

One year after my PALMS experiment began I can see the results. It is good to see and experience this success through a real-life stock purchase because I now know this system works through my own direct experience.

44

THANK YOU

I truly hope this book helps you to become a better investor too, and I want to remind you that if you believe you can do something, I guarantee you can do it.

Thank you for reading this book!

If you enjoyed this book and feel it would be helpful to other readers, please write a review on the "Stock Market Intelligence" page at Amazon.

I welcome your ideas on ways I can improve it. I want this book to be useful to you, and I welcome any feedback you share.

I appreciate your taking the time to leave a review, and I know future readers will too.

Thank you for your time.
Jeff Luke

CONNECT

If there's anything you wish you could learn about ETFs but didn't find in these pages, please send me an email and I'll try to include the material in a future edition.

You can reach me by email at jlukephoto@gmail.com

Thanks for taking the time to read this book. I appreciate your time and look forward to hearing from you.

ABOUT THE AUTHOR

Jeff Luke lives and works as a photographer and writer in Seattle, Washington. His photography has appeared in *The New York Times* and other publications worldwide.

Stock Market Intelligence is his first book about investing. Other titles include *The ETF Investor* (2020), *Winvesting* (2020), and *Smart Stocks* (2019).

His book "Animal Donut: Images & Stories" features artistic photos of animals & donuts, and you can check them out on his website: animaldonut.com and Instagram @animaldonut

He enjoys biking, photography, writing, and taking huskies Maximus and Snowy for walks along the lake.

If you have any questions or would like to connect, please email jlukephoto@gmail.com

ALSO BY JEFF LUKE

The ETF Investor (2020)

Learn to crush it with exchange-traded funds (ETFs), which are a simple way for investors of all levels of experience to instantly own a diverse stock portfolio.

Beginning with simple approaches to help investors who are just getting started investing in ETFs, this book dives deep into exploring 23 ETFs that provide a good investing foundation.

Winvesting (2020)

This book teaches you how to get started investing with index funds. This is a useful book for beginning investors who want to learn how to set up an account. It also has sections that will appeal to advanced investors who wish to improve their investment portfolios with a variety of index funds.

Smart Stocks (2019)

This book expands on the PALMS filtering system introduced in *Stock*

Market Intelligence, and it expands these investment factors for applications investing in the stocks of small companies.

NOTES

2. Accelerate Your Learning

1. Charlie Munger Talks Investment Filters. https://youtu.be/WlC40B9qZ20
2. Charlie Munger said, "The professional can't justify their existence if that's all they have to say; it's so obvious and so simple, what would they have to do with the rest of the semester?" https://youtu.be/WlC40B9qZ20

3. What Do You Understand?

1. Source: Business Wire https://www.businesswire.com/news/home/20200617005786/en/Waters-Corporation-Announces-CEO-Succession-Plan
2. Understanding Circle of Competence. Source: Forbes. https://www.forbes.com/sites/gurufocus/2015/01/02/understanding-circle-of-competence-and-knowing-the-edge-of-your-competency/#59e73be645a7
3. Understanding Circle of Competence. Source: Forbes. https://www.forbes.com/sites/gurufocus/2015/01/02/understanding-circle-of-competence-and-knowing-the-edge-of-your-competency/#59e73be645a7

5. P For Profitable

1. Source: 2018 Berkshire Hathaway Annual Letter

7. L For Loyal

1. Brand Keys Loyalty Leaders List 2017 http://brandkeys.com/wp-content/uploads/2017/10/Press-Release-2017-Loyalty-Leaders.pdf
2. Full disclosure, my car is insured by GEICO

8. M For Moat

1. YouTube Video - Nitin Nohria Interviews Jorge Paulo Lemann and Warren Buffett, intro by Larissa Maranhão: https://www.youtube.com/watch?v=Co3GFCqQInw&t=666s

9. S For Sensible Price

1. Amazon Web Services (AWS) is a subsidiary of Amazon that provides on-demand cloud computing platforms and APIs to individuals, companies, and governments, on a metered pay-as-you-go basis. Source: Wikipedia https://en.wikipedia.org/wiki/Amazon_Web_Services

2. At the time of writing, a deal has been announced in which Disney will buy a large part of Fox. The deal has not been finalized at the moment. For this reason, I have not yet added Fox to the list of Disney assets, but by the time you read this list of Disney's assets may include Fox. "Disney buys much of Fox in megamerger that will shake world of entertainment and media" The Washington Post by Stephen Zilchick December 14, 2017. Source: https://www.washingtonpost.com/news/business/wp/2017/12/14/disney-buys-much-of-fox-in-mega-merger-that-will-shake-world-of-entertainment-and-media/?utm_term=.06037bbdba3b

3. This process requires reading and work on your part. You can start with the company's annual report, and also read the company's financial reports. Watch videos about the company, talk to friends, go to stores, talk to people, do whatever it takes to get to know what the entire company would be worth to a hypothetical buyer.

4. Margin of safety is a principle of investing in which an investor buys stock only when the quoted price is far below the value of the shares. In other words, you only buy shares when the share price represents a discount to what you believe the company is worth (intrinsic value) on a "per share" basis. The difference between the intrinsic value and the quoted price is the margin of safety.

   For more information about the concept of margin of safety please see Chapter 20 of Benjamin Graham's book, "The Intelligent Investor," published by Harper & Brothers, 1949.

5. Current price is $190.09 as of this writing on December 18, 2017

6. "The Intelligent Investor" by Benjamin Graham, Harper & Brothers, 1949

7. Seth Klarman means buying something at a high price, and then the price falling abruptly, and then having to wait for years for the price to reach the original purchase price. https://novelinvestor.com/seth-klarman-speculating-humility-cycles/

8. Timeless and Time-Tested Warren Buffett Watch Predictions https://www.cnbc.com/id/34206949

11. A New Way

1. "The Intelligent Investor" by Benjamin Graham. Harper & Brothers, 1949.

12. How To Invest Today

1. "The Intelligent Investor" by Benjamin Graham and David Dodd, "Margin of Safety" by Seth Klarman, "Common Stocks for Uncommon Profits" by Phillip Fisher, and One Up on Wall Street by Peter Lynch.
2. "The Intelligent Investor" by Benjamin Graham, Harper and Brothers 1949.
3. A circle of competence is a term that Buffett uses to describe the areas in which an investor has a deep understanding. The circle does not have to include many different things. The most important aspect is that one must know the edges of ones' competency.
4. "Missing his chance to invest in Google" section of article: "Warren Buffett's Failures: 15 investing mistakes he regrets" https://www.cnbc.com/2017/12/15/warren-buffetts-failures-15-investing-mistakes-he-regrets.html
5. Jeff Bezos, Chairman and CEO of Amazon.com in the 2016 Annual Report, page 4 http://phx.corporate-ir.net/phoenix.zhtml?c=97664&p=irol-reportsannual
6. CNBC Excerpts: Billionaire Investor Warren Buffett Speaks with CNBC'S Becky Quick on "Squawk Box" Today https://edit.nbcumv.com/news/cnbc-excerpts-billionaire-investor-warren-buffett-speaks-cnbc%E2%80%99s-becky-quick-squawk-box-today
7. Jeff Bezos, Chairman and CEO of Amazon.com in the 2016 Annual Report, page 3 http://phx.corporate-ir.net/phoenix.zhtml?c=97664&p=irol-reportsannual

13. What Is A Stock?

1. Warren Buffett's shareholder letter in the 2017 Berkshire Hathaway Annual Report

14. Find Your Edge

1. Forbes Magazine: "Understanding Circle of Competence and Knowing the Edge of Your Competency" https://www.forbes.com/sites/gurufocus/2015/01/02/understanding-circle-of-competence-and-knowing-the-edge-of-your-competency/#430dcd1645a7
2. Forbes Magazine Jan 2, 2015 https://www.forbes.com/sites/gurufocus/2015/01/02/understanding-circle-of-competence-and-knowing-the-edge-of-your-competency/#5125e66145a7
3. While writing this book during the summer and fall of 2017, I did not own shares of amazon.com. On the final trading day of the year, December 29, 2017, I purchased shares of the company. Please see the chapter "Decisive on Amazon" to learn more.
4. See the chapter toward the end of this book, "Decisive on Amazon" in Part 5 for an update.
5. "One Up on Wall Street" by Peter Lynch, Simon & Schuster 1989

15. Buffett On His Edge

1. Becoming Warren Buffett (2017) TV-PG | 1h 30min | Documentary | 30 January 2017 (USA) Director Peter W. Kunhardt Writer Chris Chuang
2. Becoming Warren Buffett (2017) TV-PG | 1h 30min | Documentary | 30 January 2017 (USA) Director Peter W. Kunhardt Writer Chris Chuang
3. "GEICO'S Top Market Strategist Churning out Profits," The Washington Post, May 11, 1987 https://www.washingtonpost.com/archive/business/1987/05/11/geicos-top-market-strategist-churning-out-profits/04888c38-f2ea-4408-8621-9b98b7770cdc/
4. "GEICO'S Top Market Strategist Churning out Profits," The Washington Post, May 11, 1987 https://www.washingtonpost.com/archive/business/1987/05/11/geicos-top-market-strategist-churning-out-profits/04888c38-f2ea-4408-8621-9b98b7770cdc/

17. Focus Is Key

1. The Snowball: Warren Buffett and the Business of Life by Alice Schroeder 2009 Bantam
2. "Poor Charlie's Almanack - The Wit and Wisdom of Charles T. Munger edited by Peter D. Kaufman - The Donning Company, Publisher
3. Warren Buffett Gives Advice to Girl Scouts at Dairy Queen - YouTube Video https://www.youtube.com/watch?v=4BJfEI300rY

18. A Good Checklist

1. The Checklist Manifesto: How to Get Things Right — Picador – 2011
2. When do pilots use checklists? http://enroute.aircanada.com/en/articles/when-do-pilots-use-checklists

19. A Reliable System

1. Chapter 5, "P for Profitable" provides instructions for downloading an annual report.
2. Billionaire peers Gates and Druckenmiller warned Buffett he'd be wrong on IBM https://www.cnbc.com/2017/05/05/billionaire-peers-gates-and-druckenmiller-warned-buffett-hed-be-wrong-on-ibm.html
3. "Beating the Street" by Peter Lynch, Simon & Schuster 1994.

20. The Magic Box

1. Scott Galloway, "The Algebra of Happiness" YouTube video https://www.youtube.com/watch?v=qMW6xgPgY4s
2. https://www.valuewalk.com/charlie-munger-page/

21. Eye On Eternity

1. Quote from the YouTube video "Legacy of Ben Graham" https://youtu.be/m1WLoNEqkV4

22. Ideas From Great Investors

1. "Just a Regular Billionaire" video on YouTube: https://www.youtube.com/watch?v=P9YTKb5PgR0
2. Carol Loomis is a former Fortune Magazine journalist, author, and a longtime friend of Warren Buffett. https://en.wikipedia.org/wiki/Carol_Loomis
3. Source: 2020 Berkshire Hathaway Annual Meeting transcript.

23. We're All Indexers

1. Number of US Publicly Traded Companies falls by 50%: https://www.valuewalk.com/2018/07/number-of-us-public-companies-fall-50/

24. My Investing Mistakes

1. While this was a brash decision, it was a calculated risk. I kept my investments in the other two funds I mentioned earlier. I also had some cash in the bank. I wasn't putting my entire bet on just one spin of the roulette wheel, but I did make a big enough investment that the mistake is memorable. I learned that I did not know nearly enough about either company to make such a bold move. I thought I knew a lot because I read their annual reports, but I should have invested in companies I understood better, or just stuck with the index fund.
2. Source of Leucadia National historical stock returns: Morningstar. For those looking for historical information about Leucadia National, please note that the company changed its name to Jefferies Financial Group on May 23, 2018. Source: Businesswire.
3. What are the next-generation blood substitutes? Source: Medscape https://www.medscape.com/answers/207801-168636/what-are-the-next-generation-blood-substitutes
4. As of Jul 07, 2020 | Source: Morningstar

5. Wall Street Chiefs' Pay Doesn't Sync With Returns https://www.wsj.com/articles/wall-street-chiefs-pay-doesnt-sync-with-returns-11562580018
6. Leucadia National Corporation was renamed Jefferies Financial Group in 2018. 10-year returns for Leucadia National Corporation and White Mountain Insurance Group are as of July 23, 2018
7. I would like to point out to those readers who are interested in financial details that though I owned both Leucadia and White Mountains stock, the 10-year period ending July 23, 2018 is not my exact holding period. My realized returns are similar, however: the two stocks averaged a compound average return of 1% over the 10-year period, during which the S&P 500 returned about 10%.
8. While some 19th-century experiments suggested that the underlying premise is true if the heating is sufficiently gradual, according to contemporary biologists the premise is false: a frog that is gradually heated will jump out. Indeed, thermoregulation by changing location is a fundamentally necessary survival strategy for frogs and other ectotherms. Source: Wikipedia, The Boiling Frog
9. "Buying Berkshire Hathaway was a $200 Billion Blunder" https://www.cnbc.com/id/39710609

25. A Calm Captain

1. https://en.wikipedia.org/wiki/Chesley_Sullenberger

26. If

1. An index that represents the stock market performance of 30 of the largest companies in the United States.
2. "Wild January Stock Market Ends on a High Note" https://money.cnn.com/2016/01/29/investing/dow-january-2016-worst-month/

27. The Antifragile Investor

1. Antifragile: Things that Gain From Disorder by Nassim Nicholas Taleb.

28. Cheap Stock Trades

1. https://bebusinessed.com/history/history-of-online-stock-trading/

29. Robinhood Dreams

1. I mention Robinhood because it was the first free stock trading app I encountered, not that it's the only one, or the best one. There are other free investing

platforms like M1 Finance and likely some others that have appeared since this book's publication.

2. Benjamin Graham was the author of "The Intelligent Investor" and was Warren Buffett's professor at Columbia University and mentor. Buffett worked for Graham's company, "Graham-Newman Corporation" after graduating from Columbia. https://www.investopedia.com/articles/07/ben_graham.asp

3. YouTube Video: Legacy of Benjamin Graham https://youtu.be/m1WLoNEqkV4

4. For more on this, see the chapter titled "The Magic Box."

31. Patience

1. Berkshire Hathaway Corporation 1990 Annual Report
2. Common Stocks and Uncommon Profits by Philip Fisher, Wiley, 1957

34. Your inner scorecard

1. Warren Buffett: The Inner Scorecard. Source: Farnam Street blog https://www.f-s.blog/2016/08/the-inner-scorecard/

2. "The Snowball: Warren Buffett and the Business of Life" by Alice Schroeder, Bantam Books, 2008.

35. Buffett And Munger's Filters

1. Charlie Munger discusses investing filters: https://www.youtube.com/watch?v=WlC40B9qZ20

36. You Don't Need A Genius I.Q

1. From the forward to "The Intelligent Investor" by Benjamin Graham. Harper & Brothers, 1949.

37. Zero-Based Thinking

1. What is Zero-based thinking? http://whatis.techtarget.com/definition/zero-based-thinking-ZBT

2. Brian Tracy - Zero-Based Thinking https://www.youtube.com/watch?v=2s2at9o9yYg

3. Berkshire Hathaway's Wikipedia page. https://en.wikipedia.org/wiki/Berkshire_Hathaway

4. Zero Based Thinking: Removing Emotion from the Equation http://preneurmarketing.com/business-building/zero-based-thinking-removing-emotion-from-your-decision-making/

38. Keep It Simple

1. Charlie Munger explains how Warren Buffett outperforms the market. This video is from the 2019 Daily Journal Annual Shareholder Meeting. https://youtu.be/53vXIbsaBgw
2. Charlie Munger explains how Warren Buffett outperforms the market. This video is from the 2019 Daily Journal Annual Shareholder Meeting. https://youtu.be/53vXIbsaBgw
3. Charlie Munger at the Berkshire Hathaway 1997 Annual Meeting http://www.businessinsider.com/charlie-munger-quotes-investing-things-2016-1/#keep-it-simple-8
4. http://theinvestmentsblog.blogspot.com/2011_12_01_archive.html
5. An afternoon with Charlie Munger http://beta.morningstar.com/articles/169398/an-afternoon-with-charlie-munger.html
6. https://boundedrationality.wordpress.com/quotes/charlie-munger/

41. Thought Into Action

1.
2. Anchoring is a cognitive bias that occurs when we see a number (like a stock price) before we consider the value ourselves. The number that has been shown to us before affects our estimate, which will always be relatively close to that first number, which is called the *anchor*." Source: Facile Things https://facilethings.com/blog/en/anchoring-effect
3. "Thinking Fast and Slow" by Daniel Kahneman, 2011 Farrar, Straus and Giroux
4. Warren Buffett on CNBC's "Squawk Box" on Monday, May 1, 2017 https://www.cnbc.com/2017/05/06/warren-buffett-admits-he-made-a-mistake-on-google.html

42. Decisive On Amazon

1. From Poor Charlie's Almanack: The Wit and Wisdom of Charles T. Munger
2. In the Amazon 2016 Letter to Shareholders, CEO Jeff Bezos discussed the qualities that differentiate a company with the "Day 1" start-up mentality from those companies that make decisions slowly — what Bezos refers to as "Day 2" companies. Bezos said, "To keep the energy and dynamism of Day 1, you have to somehow make high-quality, high-velocity decisions." I believe that to invest in companies like Amazon one needs to adopt the same mindset to make high-quality, high-velocity decisions. If you wait around forever and don't ever buy

stock, that could turn out to be an expensive mistake. https://www.amazon.com/p/feature/z609g6sysxur57t

3. A buy limit order is a way to buy shares of stock at a designated price or lower. It ensures you don't pay too much when you buy shares. A buy limit order can only be executed at the limit price or lower. For example, if you want to buy a share of stock at $33 per share and it's currently selling at $40 a share, a buy limit order will only execute if the stock price falls to $33 a share or less. It only ensures that your order may execute if a pre-determined price is reached. Limit orders "limit" the price you are willing to pay when buying or selling stock, but they do not guarantee your order will be filled. A limit order is not guaranteed to execute. For more information on limit orders, see https://www.sec.gov/fast-answers/answerslimithtm.html

4. Amazon, Not Apple, to Become First Trillion Dollar Company: NYU's Galloway https://youtu.be/FuoxHXX8ZjQ?t=4m56s

5. Poor Charlie's Almanack: The Wit and Wisdom of Charles T. Munger

Made in the USA
Monee, IL
11 December 2020